The New York Times

CHANGING PERSPECTIVES

Military Service

THE NEW YORK TIMES EDITORIAL STAFF

Published in 2019 by New York Times Educational Publishing
in association with The Rosen Publishing Group, Inc.
29 East 21st Street, New York, NY 10010

First Edition

The New York Times
Alex Ward: Editorial Director, Book Development
Phyllis Collazo: Photo Rights/Permissions Editor
Heidi Giovine: Administrative Manager

Rosen Publishing
Megan Kellerman: Managing Editor
Marcia Amidon Lusted: Editor
Greg Tucker: Creative Director
Brian Garvey: Art Director

Cataloging-in-Publication Data
Names: New York Times Company.
Title: Military service / edited by the New York Times editorial staff.
Description: New York : New York Times Educational Publishing,
2019. | Series: Changing perspectives | Includes glossary and index.
Identifiers: ISBN 9781642821529 (library bound) | ISBN
9781642821512 (pbk.) | ISBN 9781642821536 (ebook)
Subjects: LCSH: United States—Armed Forces—Juvenile literature.
| United States. Air Force—Juvenile literature. | United States.
Army—Juvenile literature.
Classification: LCC UA23.M555 2019 | DDC 355.00973—dc23

Manufactured in the United States of America

On the cover: U.S. military service members in uniform;
Thinkstock Images/Stockbyte/Getty Images.

Contents

Expanding Directives and Personnel

Gender and Sexuality

CHAPTER 4

The Future of the Military and U.S. Veterans

Introduction

THE HISTORY OF MILITARY SERVICE in the United States spans over 200 years and includes 12 major wars, beginning with the American Revolution and continuing through the Iraq War. According to the U.S. Department of Veterans Affairs, a total of 41,892,128 Americans have served in the military during wartime, and many more have served during peacetime. Some have been drafted to military service in times of conflict, and others have joined the military voluntarily, to serve their country or to benefit from educational assistance and career training.

Americans have served in the four branches of the military: Army, Navy, Air Force and Marines. They have also served in the U.S. Coast Guard and in the National Guard. They have participated in conflicts on U.S. soil, such as the American Revolution and the Civil War, in far-off regions of Europe, and in Korea, Vietnam, Iraq and Afghanistan. They fought in the trenches during World War I and on the beaches of Normandy, France, during World War II.

But military service has changed a great deal from the first days of colonial militias, with Minutemen who were prepared to muster and fight in their towns with just a few minutes' notice. The weapons have changed, from muskets to automatic rifles, wagons to tanks, wooden ships to aircraft carriers and biplanes to stealth bombers. The military has seen amazing changes in technology, with guided missile systems, satellite reconnaissance, drone spy aircraft and nuclear weapons.

The military has also had to adjust to keep up with a changing social landscape. Where once military service was mostly for young white men, gradually it has come to include all races of Americans, as well as women in combat roles. Today, it is adjusting to include

Military service includes an incredibly wide range of duties, in times of both peace and war. Seen here, paratroopers from the 173rd Airborne Brigade jump onto the drop zone at Bezmer Airbase in Bulgaria, participating in military exercises with approximately 40,000 troops from 30 countries in the Black Sea Region.

openly LGBTQ service members as well. There are also ongoing concerns for immigrants — sometimes undocumented — who serve in the military prior to gaining U.S. citizenship, as well as concerns for women who seek admission to previously male-only military academies and special forces groups.

The war on terrorism and the need for increased protection and vigilance has stretched the resources of the military. After a period of time when military spending decreased, and many military bases were being closed, the U.S. government is once again spending more on the military because of possible worldwide threats and the need for a strong defensive force. But the military is having an increasingly difficult time recruiting young people to join. Although terrorist incidents such as the attacks in New York City on Sept. 11, 2001, will often cause military enlistment to increase, public attitudes toward soldiers have fluctuated widely throughout history: World War II soldiers were strongly supported, while Vietnam War soldiers and veterans faced backlash and negativity. Today, there is a strong culture of gratitude toward those who serve and defend the United States, but that does not necessarily correlate with enlistment rates.

At a 2017 "Future of War" conference, Army Chief of Staff General Mark A. Milley stated that the United States is approaching a fundamental shift in the character of war over the next 10–20 years. Battles will move from open terrain into city streets. Government diplomacy will be just as important as military equipment in handling conflicts. Future conflicts will take place not regionally, but globally. Military leaders will have to reduce the red tape involved in accomplishing many military goals. Artificial intelligence, robotic equipment and autonomous vehicles will become more and more important. Cyber-defense will also become a necessity. And as always, changing government positions will affect the availability of funding for new defense strategies, personnel and equipment.

Military service has changed greatly since George Washington led the Continental Army against the British in 1775. Today's soldiers may fight with the latest technology, side by side with women or transgender comrades in the sands of Afghanistan, but they all share one thing in common. Whether they were called up by a draft, or joined voluntarily, they have all served, and often paid with their lives, to ensure the safety and freedom of the United States.

CHAPTER 1

The Roots of the U.S. Military

Throughout its long history, the U.S. military has had both successes and failures. It has developed its own customs and culture, faced growing pains, dealt with a changing society and endured the rise and fall of attitudes toward the military. It has enjoyed times of great patriotism, and it has suffered budget cuts and a poor reputation with civilians. But even so, these growing pains have been responsible for much of what the military has accomplished.

The United States Army: Report of Major General Scott

SPECIAL TO THE NEW YORK TIMES | DEC. 15, 1852

Headquarters of the Army, Washington, Nov. 22, 1852

Hon. C. M. Conrad, Secretary of War

SIR: The following returns from the Adjutant General's Office accompany this general report:

1. Organization of the Army as established by law, marked A.

2. General return of the Army, showing the actual numbers borne on the rolls, B.

3. Distribution of the troops in the Eastern Division, C.

4. Distribution of the troops in the Western Division, D.

5. Distribution of the troops in the Third or Pacific Division, E.

6. Statement of the number of recruits enlisted from Oct. 1, 1851, to Sept. 30, 1852, F.

During the past twelve months the troops on the frontiers have been actively employed, and have had several sharp combats with parties of Indians in Texas, New Mexico, and California. All, however, is now quiet, and it is hoped the judicious distribution of the forces made by the commanders in those quarters may prevent any further outbreaks. Eight companies of the rifle regiment, withdrawn from Oregon last year, having been recruited and re-mounted, were ordered to Texas, where an additional mounted force was much needed. For the defence of the frontiers of that State there are now, under the orders of Brevet Major Gen. Smith, fourteen companies of cavalry, two companies of artillery, with three regiments and two companies of infantry — in all, forty-eight companies. The three infantry regiments are distributed along an exterior cordon of posts, in advance of the white settlements, and stretching from Eagle Pass, on the Rio Grande, to Preston, on the Red river. The remainder of the force is posted on the Rio Grande, below Eagle Pass, and along a second line interior to the first. By this arrangement the mounted troops are foraged more economically and with greater facility, and are in position to move promptly to any assailed point of the first line.

The force in New-Mexico consists of nine companies of dragoons, two of artillery, and one regiment (ten companies) of infantry. Several new posts have been recently established in this Territory, near the heart of the Indian country, and appear to have had the effect of awing the warlike tribes into quietness.

The hostile disposition manifested by the Indians in California and Oregon requiring that our troops in that quarter should be reinforced, the fourth regiment of infantry was withdrawn from the Northern lakes and ordered thither. The force under Brevet Brig. Gen. Hitchcock, who commands the Pacific division, will soon consist of three companies of dragoons, five companies of artillery, and two regiments (twenty companies) of infantry — in all twenty-eight companies.

Several changes in the station of the troops within this division have been made during the year. The post at the mouth of the Gila has been reoccupied with a garrison of three companies. This post will exercise a salutary check on the Yuma Indians, the most warlike tribe in California, and who have hitherto greatly harassed the emigrants passing through their country by the southern route to the Pacific. The whole of the fourth infantry, eight companies of which have already arrived out, is to be stationed in Oregon and Northern California — the headquarters, with four companies, at Vancouver; one company at the Dalles of the Columbia river; and the remainder of the regiment so distributed as to guard and keep open the communications between Oregon and California.

The other movements of troops, of less importance, may be thus briefly stated: A portion of the Fourth Artillery, sent from the seaboard to replace the Fourth Infantry on the Northern lakes, and two companies of the Second Artillery, sent from Charleston harbor to Florida, to meet the possibility of difficulties in that quarter, growing out of the contemplated removal thence of a remnant of Seminoles, to the country assigned them west of the Arkansas.

THE RECRUITING SERVICE.

The recruiting service has been conducted with the usual success, the number of men enlisted being 4,174. The officers engaged in this branch of the service have shown a commendable zeal in the performance of their duties. Their accounts have, in general, been promptly rendered and the expenditures judiciously made.

The attention of recruiting officers has been repeatedly called to the subject of minors, in order to guard against the enlistment of any except in strict accordance with law. The general regulations, in conformity therewith, prohibit such enlistments without the written consent of the parent, master, or guardian of the minor, if he have any, and if he affirm that he has neither, he is required, before acceptance, to have a guardian appointed according to law, to give the written consent. With all the care and scrutiny thus exercised, many minors, whose appearance indicates full age, but who turn out to be less by 10, 15, and even 20 months, impose themselves on the recruiting officers. This is almost daily shown by applications from parents and guardians to the Secretary of War, who, on proof of minority, is compelled to grant discharges under the 5th section of the act "making appropriations for the support of the army," &c., approved September 28, 1850. To guard the public interest against the vexations and great pecuniary loss attending such frauds, additional legislation would seem to be necessary. It is accordingly suggested that the minor who thus seeks to make money by imposing himself on the service, should either be compelled to serve out the term of enlistment or the offence be made punishable before a civil court.

The third section of the act of June 17, 1850, "to increase the rank and file of the army and to encourage enlistments," having almost entirely failed to effect its purposes, may advantageously be repealed. Very few men enter the service for the first time at our more distant stations; and an ample bounty is provided for the soldier who reenlists, by the twenty-ninth section of the act "to increase the present military establishment," &c., approved July 5, 1838.

FARM CULTURE.

So far, farm culture by the troops, as directed by general order No. 1, Jan. 8, 1851 (a copy of which was appended to my last annual report), has not fulfilled the desired objects. In Texas, California, and Oregon nothing has been attempted, in consequence of the troops in those departments being constantly employed either in the pursuit of marauding Indians, or in the establishment of new posts to hold them in check and protect the frontier settlements. In New-Mexico but little was accomplished during the past year, and the outlay far exceeded the receipts. Better results, doubtless, may hereafter be expected there, particularly as it has been found necessary to employ, as farmers, hired citizens. At the distant posts on the Western plains cultivation failed entirely. It will perhaps be expedient, looking to the encouragement of population in the neighborhood of military posts, to discontinue the system. Besides the protection gained, a main inducement with emigrants to settle near a military station is to find a ready market for their surplus produce, which inducement would be taken away if the public farms were successful. It is found, moreover, that troops cannot be kept actively engaged in military duties, and maintain discipline, if required to engage in cultivation beyond kitchen gardens.

REVISION OF THE RULES AND ARTICLES OF WAR.

Congress (Sept. 20, 1776,) borrowed entire from the mother country the statutory code for our Revolutionary army, which stood without material change down to April 10, 1806, when the present rules and articles were reenacted upon a revision made in one of the military committees of Congress. The revision gave a cast and form entirely new to the previous code, and embraces material changes and discrepancies — each a blunder — the effect of the excessive low state of every kind of military knowledge in the United States at that period. It is recommended that the whole subject now be referred to a board of officers, to report a new revision to be laid before Congress.

For the codes of 1776 and 1806, see *Hetzel's Military Laws*, p. 13, &c., and p. 107, &c.

TACTICAL INSTRUCTION FOR THE MILITIA.

By existing laws, the militia are required to observe the systems of instruction provided for the regular army; and yet no provision has been made for furnishing them with the necessary systems, although some nine million of dollars have been appropriated in the last forty years toward *arming* them. Without books to teach their use, the arms themselves are of little value. Hence, it is again recommended that the books be supplied. The additional annual expense need not exceed $20,000, and that only for a few years. See the remarks on this subject in my last Annual Report.

MILITARY ASYLUM.

For the progress made in carrying out the beneficent intentions of Congress, as expressed in the act of March, 1852, see the recent report of the Board, created by that act, addressed to the War Department of Congress.

RETIRED LIST FOR SUPERANNUATED AND DISABLED OFFICERS.

See the remarks on this subject in my last Annual Report. The necessity for some such measure has greatly increased since the Mexican war, the number of officers of the junior grades wounded in that war having swelled the invalid list, which previously consisted almost exclusively of officers of the senior grades, disabled by the infirmities of age. The creation of such a list ought not to be mistaken for an extension of the pension system. The officers who would be placed on it are already in the receipt of full pay without performing any duty. The system so often recommended would retire them on reduced compensation, promote efficient officers in their stead, and this greatly contribute to the good of the service, without any new imposition on the Treasury.

PROPOSED INCREASE OF CAVALRY.

The cavalry force now authorized is inadequate, by the demonstration of experience, to the wants of the service. No troops are generally so efficient against Indians, and the immense extent of our frontiers requires that at least one more regiment of horse should be added to the establishment. The number of privates allowed to companies of all arms should in no case fall below sixty-four, with a sliding scale upwards to eight-four, at the discretion of the Executive.

PROPOSED EXTENSION OF THE PENSION SYSTEM.

It would seem but just that the pension laws provided for the navy should be extended to the army. No reason is seen for the discrimination between these kindred branches of the public service. The pensions in both cases come out of the general fund; and as both share common dangers, and undergo equal vicissitudes in the discharge of duties, the same rewards should be appointed to each. The widows and orphans of deceased naval officers, seamen, and, marines receive five-year pensions, renewable every five years, whether the deaths occurred in battle or were caused by disease contracted in service, while the widows of army officers receive pensions only when their husbands have been killed in action, and then but for five years, and the period has never been extended. Widows of the enlisted men (non-commissioned officers and privates) of the army receive no pensions, no matter what the circumstances, although the laws allow pensions to the widows and orphans of volunteers (whether officers or privates) who may have been killed, or have died from any cause, while in service. Such unequal legislation ought surely to be corrected, and no time could be more appropriate than the present. The five year pensions granted to the widows, &c. of the Mexican war have just expired, or are about expiring. These relicts and widows of gallant officers are, almost without an exception, in the humblest circumstances. The subject of pensions is well represented in a report, dated Jan. 7, 1846, made by the Committee on Military Affairs of the Senate. See Senate Documents No 43, 3d volume, 1st session, 29th Congress; also (hereto annexed) extracts from my annual reports dated Nov. 22, 1841, and Nov. 26, 1846.

I have the honor to remain, sir, with high respect, your most obedient servant,

Winfield Scott

EXTRACT FROM ANNUAL REPORT
FROM HEADQUARTERS OF THE ARMY
Washington, Nov. 22, 1841

"I beg leave to recall attention to some provision of law in favor of widows and orphans of regular officers who have died or may die in consequence of wounds received or diseases contracted in service — there being such provision already made in behalf of the widows and orphans of navy, volunteer, and militia officers dying under such circumstances. Indeed the whole subject of army pensions to widows and orphans and to disabled officers requires equitable revision."

EXTRACT FROM ANNUAL REPORT
FROM HEADQUARTERS OF THE ARMY
New-York, Nov. 26, 1846

"Our pension system, including allowances to widows and children — interesting alike to regulars, volunteers and militia men, disabled and in service, and to their families when the officers and men die of wounds or other disabilities — is the poorest in all Christendom. Please see *Cross's* or *Hetzel's Mil. Laws*, following the reference of the index under the heads, 'Pensions to invalids,' and 'widows and orphans, provisions for.' 1. The limitation to half *pay*, excluding half *subsistence*; 2. To the half pay of *Lieutenant colonel*, [$30 a month.] no matter how much higher the rank of the disabled or deceased officer, [and less and less for inferior grades;] 3. Requiring the *highest* rate of disability to entitle the officer or man to receive even that sort of *half pay*; and 4. The limitation to *five* years, in respect to both widows and orphans — are all disreputable to our statue book and civilization. I trust the whole system may be liberally revised."

The Dwindling of the Army and Its Causes

BY THE NEW YORK TIMES | SEPT. 22, 1907

Col. Heistand tells why there are so few enlistments and points to reforms that should be made. One source of trouble is dissatisfaction with company commanders; then the pay is too small.

WITH EIGHTY MILLIONS of people defended by a standing army of about 40,000 men, it is not surprising that there is a public interest in the problem to know why this small number of regulars cannot be induced to appreciate the honor of carrying a musket and a sword. It has been brought forcibly to public notice recently that the powers in Washington have been embarrassed by a deficient spirit, which, though hard to define, relates to the pomp and glory of man's equipment.

Col. H. O. S. Heistand, Military Secretary of the Department of the East, has been absorbing the literature which the commanders of the various departments exchange about this time in pamphlet form. These paper-covered books contain the reports of the commanding officers upon their own departments. As contributors to the history of war they are merely a sad index of what might happen if war were declared. Briefly, while they indorse the personnel of the army, they are unanimously critical of the common soldier.

And yet, unless the enlistments increase, the common soldier will become most painfully uncommon, as rare a kind as the Museum of Natural History ever put stuffing into.

Col. Heistand fearlessly outlined several reasons for this, chief among which it is well to consider in statistical ratio.

Why there are no enlistments:

1. The pay is too small.
2. The chief duties of the service are non-military.

3. The character of enlisted men is not severely investigated at recruiting offices.

4. The army posts require a Service Corps to do camp chores, thereby permitting the recruit to wear the uniform they expected to wear.

5. The detail-draught upon officers of the line regiments causes continuous changing of company commanders.

6. The non-commissioned officers are the most deserving of higher pay.

"But, how are these matters to be remedied?" Col. Heistand was asked.

"I have reason to believe very strongly that the President is personally very much concerned about the embarrassments of the army service, and that, when the next term of Congress opens, he will find a way to restore the army to its best state of efficiency."

"But the President can only refer this matter to Congress."

"Not at all! Congress has relegated the power of command over the service to the President, with authority to increase the strength of the army to 100,000 men or less, according to his discretion. It rests entirely with the demands of the President whether the present strength is increased to that number."

"Such an increase would require a large appropriation from Congress?"

"Of course, and Congress is very properly jealous of the people's money. But, I believe, that, if the case is put before them plainly, with the President's recommendation, that Congress will supply the necessary funds. I have observed that Congress is always fair-minded, and if it can be convinced that the people's interests are to be served by an efficient system of military defense, there will be no delay in accomplishing the means. An important step, I consider the most important of all, was taken when Mr. Taft recently made a request for an increase of five hundred officers."

One of the significant features of the present inefficiency of the army service was explained by an ex-soldier in the following way.

INCOMPETENCE OF OFFICERS.

"I believe that the main cause of dissatisfaction among the men is due to the incompetence of the company commanders," he said.

"They are usually West Point graduates too young to have any knowledge of men or how to manage them. There is a human nature to contend with in the army, as in other degrees of life, and a company commander should have a knowledge of men, a quick perception of their differences in temperament, their limitations of intelligence, their inward possibilities. As it is now, there is not the slightest harmony between these young officers and the soldiers they command, with the inevitable result of such a breach between men — a complete indifference, and often bad feeling that leads to severe discipline and a military prison.

"By the time these young officers have gained some knowledge of human nature the mischief has been done, and though their promotion has been made the companies they have left behind have lost courage in their military prospects, and they do not re-enlist.

"Then again, the pay is too small. The soldier's day off is one of the most distressing events of his service, because he is usually broke. There is nothing for him to do but lay around, utterly discouraged with his condition, and he doesn't care what happens to him. On pay day, necessarily, he falls into temptation, and then it is all up with him. At least that is my observation during my term of service."

This faithful transcript of the soldier's temperament in time of peace points out one thing clearly, that the influence of the officers over the men, being strictly impersonal, makes the army service a round of technical obedience without the savor of human elements that make life worth living.

Even Col. Heistand agreed in a measure with the views expressed by the ex-soldier.

"Owing to the constant changing of company commanders, the soldiers have no chance to benefit by the association of their officers," he said.

"In the same way the officers are hampered in any effort they may make to exercise a paternal influence over their men. A company commander should be a father to his men; he should know them, each one according to his peculiarities, to his nature. He should know the weaknesses, the temper, the meanness, the manner of this one and that one, so that by watchful care and personal interest in every man under him he could insure the efficiency of them all in a body.

"An officer can be a father to his men, but under the present shortage of officers they are never in one place long enough to become intimately acquainted with the character of their men.

"Of course, I must confess that the young men who are in the rank and file of the army to-day as a whole are deficient in those qualities that go to make good soldiers. They are not of the highest type of intelligence; there seems to be something wrong with their reasoning powers, their perceptions of integrity and self-control."

"That is the fault of the recruiting officers?"

"Well, a recruiting officer is appointed to get recruits, and if an able-bodied, robust-looking youngster applies for enlistment, perhaps the recruiting officer is not so particular about the applicant's references. It is often very difficult to investigate them, too. The result is that the personnel of the regiments are not up to the standard of men required and expected in Washington."

"Once enlisted, are the men disappointed?"

"I fancy that there are very few haphazard enlistments. The young men who join the army do so to-day solely with a view to the pay, and after very careful consideration. Doubtless the pomp and glory of the uniform, which is exhibited in pretty colors on the recruiting posters, has a good deal to do with the young man's choice.

INCREASE OF PAY NEEDED.

"Consequently, when he reaches the post, and is kept at work that is entirely non-military, such as cleaning barracks, sweeping, scrubbing, and other menial duties, dressed in clothes quite different from those that he expected to shine in day and night, he feels that it is an empty glory after all to serve the flag in the character of a street cleaner, and he becomes disgusted.

"In a great measure I think he is right. What we need is a general service corps in the army to do the chores, so that the enlisted man may enjoy the benefits of his enlistment, which are the brass buttons, the musket, and the full regalia of his military rank."

"You would favor increased pay?"

"I think if the $13 a month were raised to $15, it would make a great difference in the number of enlistments. I should especially favor increased pay, however, for the non-commissioned officers, as an inducement for men to remain in the service until, by promotion, they felt that it paid, because after all, the pay is at the bottom of all enlistments to-day.

"So long as the present prosperity continues, it will be next to impossible to get recruits, unless the pay is increased."

"The number of desertions is due to lack of pay?"

"So long as the public is in sympathy with the deserter there will be desertions. The public view a soldier's desertion much as they view their individual desertion of obligations among themselves. Desertion doesn't mean all that the United States Army considers it, either to the soldier himself or the public.

"The soldier looks at it as a man does who 'quits his job,' but Uncle Sam insists upon the seriousness of an oath. In civil life an oath is mumbled before a notary and the expedient of the moment is served without a full realization of its consequences.

"The army tries to administer the oath to a recruit with more ceremony, but nine cases out of ten its importance is only half appreciated, only half understood.

"Then again, many deserters get away altogether, and only a small percentage of them is brought back for court-martial. This is because public sentiment does not sustain the sacredness of the oath taken by a recruit, and is ready to assist the deserter."

"There are more re-enlistments for foreign service than any other?"

"Because one year's foreign service counts for two years in the record of retirement lists. A man on home service must serve thirty years before he gets his pension, while a man on foreign service requires only fifteen years to accomplish his retirement on pension.

"There are many ways in which an efficient soldier can increase his pay. I know of one man who is drawing $112 a month — but he is a master electrician, and there are side issues by which he earns through personal skill and competence."

Of the 183 prisoners on Governors Island at present, a majority of them are long-term prisoners, and yet, as Col. Heistand pointed out, they were there largely through a misconception of the importance of the oath they had taken when entering the service. There was also something to be said of the decline in modern standards of the true sportsman's instinct that prevails in the navy, and should exist in the army — but does not.

THE QUESTION OF MARKSMANSHIP.

When Col. Heistand was shown the adverse criticisms that Commander Sims of the Navy Department had made of the shooting done by the artillery coast defences at a moving target, he hastily picked at random from his basket two recent reports of gun practice at Fort Heath and Fort Strong near Boston.

At Fort Strong the record showed that during a gun practice at a moving target between three and four miles distant, out of six shots being fired in a little over three minutes four had hit the mark immediately after orders to cease firing were recorded. Five record shots showed a total deviation in range of two yards from the centre of impact. Of these six shots four were absolutely "line" shots, the other two having a lateral direction of two yards each from the line.

At Fort Heath the records showed that six shots hit the centre of impact, on a plate of the thickness of battleship armor below the water line, three miles distant, moving at a speed of four or five miles.

"I think that speaks for itself that our coast defenders can shoot," said Co. Heistand, warmly, "but I regret that anything should be said in criticism of either branch of the National service of an irritating nature."

Put War Service on Men of Class 1, Urges Crowder

SPECIAL TO THE NEW YORK TIMES | JAN. 4, 1918

WASHINGTON, JAN. 3, 1918 — The large reservoirs of man power available in the United States for use against Germany are disclosed, on the basis of recent surveys, in a report made public tonight by Major Gen. Enoch Crowder, Provost Marshal General, who states his conviction that, in all probability, it will be possible to meet America's military needs by calling to the colors hereafter only the men included in Class 1 of draft registrants.

General Crowder estimates that the men in this classification accepted for service will reach 1,000.000. By amending the draft law so as to include all men who have reached their twenty-first birthday since June 5, 1917, and will hereafter reach that age, General Crowder believes that at least 700,000 men can be added yearly to the available class. For that reason he thinks that there is no immediate necessity of going beyond Class J in future drafts.

Much has been said about raising or lowering the draft age limits. General Crowder is not at this time in favor of doing this. In the interest of fair distribution of the military burden, however, he proposes that the quotas of States or districts be determined hereafter on the basis of the number of men in Class 1, and not upon population.

Class 1 comprises single men without dependent relatives, married men who have habitually failed to support their families, who are dependent upon wives for support or not usefully engaged, and whose families are supported by incomes independent of their labor, unskilled farm laborers, unskilled industrial laborers, registrants by or in respect of whom no deferred classification is claimed or made, registrants who fail to submit questionnaire and in respect. of whom no deferred classification is claimed or made, and all registrants not included in any other division of the schedule.

SURFACE OF POWER NOT SCRATCHED.

General Crowder asserts that the surface of our man power has not been scratched, and that "unless we are to confess a national inefficiency, shameful before the nations of the world, we shall solve these problems without controversy."

General Crowder gives these figures of the draft results:

Registrants.	Number.	Ratio P.C.
Total	9,586,508	100
Not called by boards	6,503,550	67.84
Called by boards	3,082,949	32.16

Of the men called by boards, 252,294 failed to appear, being 8.18 per cent. Commenting on these, General Crowder expresses the opinion that there were not more than 50,000 "real slackers."

Up to late December only 5,870 arrests had been made of those who had sought to evade registration, and of that number 2,263 were released after having registered. There remain only 2,095 cases to be prosecuted. The report says that in the final analysis of the records it will be shown that only .000026 per cent of the men within draft age evaded registration.

A total of 1,057,363 men have been certified for service and 687,000 were named in the first call. The Provost Marshal General has been ready to supply percentages of this quota more rapidly than the War Department has been able to clothe and equip the men.

General Crowder finds that the first draft surpassed the expectations of friends of the selective draft idea. He pays a high tribute to the thousands of civilians who gave ungrudging service to making the plan a success, and to the high patriotism of the American people as a whole.

"At the President's call," he says, "all ranks of the nation, reluctantly entering the war, nevertheless instantly responded to the first call of the nation with a vigorous and unselfish cooperation that submerged all individual interest in a simple endeavor toward the consummation of the national task. I take it that no great national project was ever attempted, with so complete a reliance upon the voluntary co-operation of citizens for its execution."

Discussing the question of the enlargement of the age limits for compulsory military service, the Provost Marshal General says:

"A pronounced majority of the boards favor some enlargement, but there is great diversity of opinion as to the proper age limit. Nineteen and 33 are perhaps the limits most frequently suggested, but some recommend 40 or 45 years as the upper limit. There is a distinctly stronger demand for raising the maximum age than for lowering the minimum.

"The reason given for advocating this enlargement is the fact that there are many good men under and over the present limits who could more easily be spared than an equal number within the limits.

"The following additional suggestions are made by a number of boards: (1) That young men who were under age should come within the law when they reach the minimum draft age; (2) that young men of 38 or 19 should be enrolled and trained, so as to be ready for active service immediately upon attaining draft age.

"It is obvious that we are at the threshold of this problem in our further provisions for the conduct of the war, and that a wise foresight should be employed in settling it.

NUMBER OF AVAILABLE MEN.

"The two most important preliminary inquiries are: What are the numbers of available men in the additional age groups? Which groups can we least afford to draw from? The available numbers are as follows:

MALE POPULATION AVAILABLE, 1918.

	Numbers.
31-45 years, both inclusive, (est.)	10,683,249
21-30 years, both inclusive, not yet called	6,503,559
18-20 years, both inclusive, (est.)	3,087,063
Arriving at age 21 between June, 1917, and June, 1918, (est.)	1,000,000

"Inasmuch as most (96 per cent) of the 18-20 group are not married and most (77 per cent) of the age 31-45 are married, it will serve sufficiently the purpose to estimate the number of single persons available in each of the groups, and then to take the probable number of acceptances as shown by the percentage of acceptances in the first draft. This estimated result is as follows:

PROBABLE ACCEPTABLE MEN IN AGE GROUPS

	Gross Number.	Prob. Per C't. of Acceptables.	Net Numbers.
Single males, 31-40, (estimated)	3,525,472	39.41	1,389,388
Single males, 21-30 not yet called	3,354,086	39.41	1,321,848
Single males, 18-20, (estimated)	2,963,581	39.41	1,167,947
Single males arriving at age 21 (estimated)	960,000	39.41	378,336
Total.......................	10,803,139	....	4,257,516

GROUNDS FOR PREFERENCE.

"In considering the grounds of preferences for the two groups not now liable to service conflicting considerations meet us. The younger men are generally deemed to make the soundest and most pliable military material. On the other hand, the older men are more likely to yield in large numbers the occupational skill so necessary in the varied composition of the modern army. Moreover, under the rational selective service system, which seems to distribute the burden equally among the willing and unwilling, it is important, if not essential, to include the older men, because a smaller proportion of them is likely to enlist —

that is, to enter the army voluntarily, without waiting for the call of the law. If the age limit were not enlarged to include the older men for raising the needed numbers, too large a proportion of the younger and more aggressively patriotic men would be withdrawn from civil life, thus unduly injuring the coming generation.

"In view, however, of the considerable number of men already available under the law, the main reason for enlarging the age limits at this time is to distribute the burden more equally, in preparation for a later situation of need that may arise. From this point of view the extension might well be both upward and downward by way of a registration of all ages from 19 to 21 and 31 to 45.

"In any event, the greatest caution should be exercised not to interfere with the technical training of the younger group of men. The higher training should be protected from undue inroads, for it is there that the practical sciences are being developed. Both war and industry must be able to count upon a continuous and ample supply of trained young men. The experience of continental countries here has its lessons for us.

"A wise expedient would be, (if the age limits are lowered to 18 or 19,) (1) to require every technical student in a recognized college to enter the enlisted Reserve Corps and to relieve him from call by a local board during the completion of his course; (2) to require every such student to take a course of military instruction and drill for each of such years, or to enter an officers' training camp during the Summer; (3) to appropriate the sums necessary to provide military instruction end drill at every college furnishing a unit of 100 men. By this means the vital demand for educated young men could be filled and at the same time their preparation for military service, when needed, could be insured."

POSSIBILITIES OF CLASS 1.

In another chapter of his report dealing with "the incoming age of 21 and the attained age of 30," General Crowder says:

"No human mind can forecast the resultant numbers In Class 1, but (as the roughest guess based on the experiences of the first draft) it is estimated that Class 1 will comprise a list of physically acceptable men in number close to 1,000,000 — enough for any call in present prospect. Whether this guess be justified in practice or not it can be announced as the policy and belief of this office trial in all probability it will be possible to fill our military's need's without ever invading any class more deferred than Class 1.

"It is perfectly demonstrable that the fostering of our industrial and agricultural institutions requires the deferment, not of the younger men, who have not yet become integrated with the domestic, industrial, or agricultural life of the nation, but rather of men who have passed beyond their majority and who have assumed domestic, industrial or agricultural relations which demand their discharge from the obligations of military service. Therefore, presuming that the military needs of the nation should require more men than those who within the present draftable ages, and under the present rules would be in Class 1, the problem would instantly present itself whether it were better to include the deferred Classes or to add another class of younger men.

"It is not difficult to find that the relations of a man to the war industries of a nation are sufficient to defer his call to voluntary service and in his place to send another man to a stern and vicarious sacrifice. But it is much more difficult to reach the conclusion that either the interests of the nation or the interests of the favored man are sufficient to justify sending forth in the place of a college student a less fortunate youth at the imminent and great peril of life — not because he is better fitted to defend his country, (for admittedly such is not the case,) but because the national life has vouchsafed him fewer opportunities. Yet that idea is rampant in the nation. It Is unfair and unjustly partial. Human lives and destinies are at stake. There is too great a disposition to weaken on this ground, and the sooner the nation come to an exact realization of the issues involved, that sooner will the powerful disposition of high but single-minded educators be opposed in this regard.

"The inclusion of the class of those arriving at the age of 21 should add yearly at least 700,000 undeferred men to the available class, and with such an addition there is certainly no immediate necessity of going beyond Class 1 in future drafts. This is a consummation most to be desired. It removes from consideration the most troublesome problems of the draft and places us in a most enviable position among belligerent nations.

OVER 76,000 ALIENS VOLUNTEERED.

Tables accompanying the report show many striking results of the draft. Of the 457,713 called up for examination 76,545 were certified for military service, having voluntarily waived their right to exemption as aliens and in effect volunteered for the battle for democracy. Even of the 381,168 exempted, 40 per cent went out on other grounds than their alien status.

Of the men examined, 730,756, or 23.7 per cent, were rejected for physical reasons. That, it is pointed out, shows an encouraging improvement in the physical condition of the young men of the nation since the civil war days, for at that time the draft authorities rejected 32 per cent of all men called on physical grounds.

About half of all the men called, or 1,560,570, claimed exemption. The claims of 78 per cent of these were granted, showing in the opinion of officials that very few fraudulent claims were filed. Of those exempted, 74 per cent were released because of dependent relatives, 20 per cent because they claimed alien birth and nationality, and only 6 per cent on vocational grounds.

Dolling Up Our Army: Back to Blue and Gold Braid for Our Olive Drab Fighting Men — Perhaps

BY THE NEW YORK TIMES | MAY 13, 1923

MILITARY CIRCLES FOR several months have been greatly interested, even agitated, over the matter of a change in the cut and color of army uniforms. The question is whether or not the army will return to the before-the-war blue dress or remain in the present olive drab. Not only the Regular Army but the National Guard and the officers of the Organized Reserves are involved, since the idea persists that the uniform for all parts of the service shall be identical. Discussion by officers and men has been lively, and the service papers have contained a great deal of comment pro and con.

"One wonders," said an officer of the old school, "whether we are to have an army of soldiers who are proud of their profession or an army of men who wear a uniform in the same way that it is worn by police and mailmen. Are we to remain soldiers in the same sense that we have been, or are we to wear a uniform while on duty and then immediately seek the incognito of civilian clothing? This is the practice which is being developed by the one uniform now authorized."

The United States Army is the only military organization, not omitting our own navy and Marine Corps, which does not have at least one, usually several, uniforms for different occasions. It is under the same handicap that civilians would be if limited to clothes of one cut and color. Yet there is a section of army opinion which views with disfavor the adoption of further uniforms. This in face of the fact that traditionally one of the most attractive things about military service, from both the inside and outside, has in the past been the color and brilliance of the uniform.

Officers of higher rank deplore the vogue which the present uniform regulations encourage of wearing one suit the entire day. This practice, it is pointed out by one general officer, is neither pleasant nor the habit of gentlemen. The answer of the shavetails, of course, might well be that it is difficult to retain all the habits ascribed to gentlemen, on seventeen hundred yearly, particularly if the habits of gentlemen include marriage.

The adoption of another uniform obviously would cost money, would put many junior officers in debt. On this point a "Lieutenant of Infantry," writing to one of the service publications recently, says:

"A change in clothing which is still decidedly military cannot help but increase the morale of the army. A few hundred dollars more or less when you are in debt will make little difference."

Advocates of the blue uniform urge that it would add to the comfort of the wearer and prove of advantage in the matter of personal appearance by providing a change of uniforms for special events. They say that many enlist in the Marine Corps rather than in the army because the marine uniforms are more attractive.

Modern dress uniforms are not, as some might fancy, the creations of the Quartermaster General's wife, nor of his tailor. The cut, the gold lace, the braid, even the arrangement of the buttons, have usually to the officers and men who wear them a historical and sentimental significance. Military men, since the first uniform was issued by a grouchy Swedish supply sergeant, have been proud of that insignia attached to it which referred to some previous glory of the outfit. They are loath to see these abolished by mere regulation. Probably when Gustavus Adolphus, about 1623, hit upon the happy idea of giving his legions sashes of different colors he did not realize the controversy which was to follow. He was the man who first uniformed his fighters by giving each brigade a sash of different color to be worn in battle.

Curiously, the enemies of Gustavus Adolphus did not at once follow his lead, and for a long time the only troops boasting any uniform at all were his. Some smaller lords and princes did have retainers garbed in their colors, but these bands were small and scattered. When those old boys went to war in earnest they called for their peasants, who pulled the old family sword or meat-axe off the wall and hung it on over the Middle Age equivalent of overalls.

Usually the only insignia by which one side could be distinguished from the other was the banner of the leader. This was raised as the rallying point and must be protected at all costs, for when it went down or was lost there was a possibility of the fight going merrily on, good farm hands impartially "beaning" unknown friend and foe. The gathering of embattled men about their colors and the fate which overtook those who became separated from them caused the standard to be held in almost holy regard by the soldiery and the sacredness of the flag remains with us as a heritage.

Even the scarf or sash period in uniforms was not much further along. At Edgehill, during the great English rebellion, a squire, elaborately disguising himself with a cast-off orange sash, went unhindered through the ranks of the Parliamentary army and recovered the lost royal standard from the hands of Essex's own Secretary. In France at the same time the general character of the clothing and accoutrements to be worn by the military was regulated by royal decree, but this was hardly uniform as we use the word.

In 1645 the British Parliament raised an army for its very own — the first national army. In this fighting force for the first time the Colonels were officials and not more or less independent proprietors responsible for the clothing of their men. This army was clothed all in red coats and gray breeches. The coats were faced with regimental colors, establishing a custom in uniform manufacture which has lasted nearly 300 years. Although distinctive in color, these uniforms consisted of the ordinary garments, cut in the civilian mode of the period — simple coat, waistcoat, breeches, stockings and shoes or boots. About this time the helmet for infantry disappeared and a floppy felt hat took its place. The use of this hat became almost universal. Its broad rim was fastened up on one side at first, later on both sides. Thus it become the forebear of our present Generals' and Admirals' full dress chapeaux. Later still it was fastened up in three places, resulting in the cocked hat of Colonial times and modern slang.

The great variety of uniforms which spread over Europe about 1700 can be traced to the various local and national costumes. Military units were as a rule drawn from one region, and the garb of the local folk, usually their Sunday go-to-meetin' clothes, were with some variations, made the uniform.

Shortly after the Colonies had decided to form a Continental Army a general order was issued from the headquarters at Cambridge that "the Colonels of the new establishment shall as soon as possible deposit with the Quartermaster General the uniforms their respective regiments." Naturally these new American Colonels modeled the uniforms of their outfits on those of their favorite European outfits. At first most of them bore the imprint of the British service. Later in the war uniforms in the Continental forces grew scarce and many units were garbed in woodsmen's costume. Many soldiers of an older school must have groaned when gazing upon their commands clad in hunting shirts and leather breeches.

The old method of having uniforms of one color with facings and cuffs designating organization was attempted a little later in the war, but owing to lack of cloth and other reasons this was never wholly successful. Washington at one time could not tell his Generals' rank by their uniforms and was forced to issue an order that "Majors and Brigadiers General shall wear from the right shoulder across the breast, above the waistcoat, a red ribband." He even had to amend this with "Majors General shall wear a broad ribband and Brigadiers General a narrower ribband, aides-de-camp a green ribband."

From this the present sashes worn by general officers of our forces descended.

At another time the Commander-in-Chief in an order stated that in some outfits he had difficulty in distinguishing junior officers from non-coms and soldiers. This he had to correct by prescribing more insignia for the former. Evidently in those days the shavetails were not as fond of putting on the dog as they have become.

Later in the war the uniforms were as far as possible blue, with facings and cuffs of regimental colors. Certain colors were finally assigned to each arm or branch and the facings were made to conform with these, some small bit of decoration from the older regimental colors being retained. A survival is the green cuffs on the prewar dress coats of the Third Cavalry, inherited from the Third Dragoons. Those late Revolutionary uniforms were great affairs. What of the direct European touch was in them was mostly French. The chevrons now worn by officers on their overcoats, by marine officers on dress uniforms and by non-coms of that service on their blues have been handed down direct from Lafayette's troops.

The custom of having distinctive badges for old-timers among the enlisted men to show their length of service is an idea of Washington's. His first order on the subject was issued from his Newburgh headquarters on August 7, 1782, and might almost be that in force now. It reads: "Honorary badges of distinction are to be conferred upon the veteran non-commissioned officers and soldiers of the army who have served more than three years with bravery, fidelity and good conduct. For this purpose a narrow piece of white cloth is to be fixed on the left arm of uniform coats. Non-commissioned officers and soldiers who have served more than six years are to be distinguished by two pieces of cloth, set parallel to each other in a similar form." In 1920, nearly 140 years later, a very similar regulation was adopted, enlisted men now wearing an olive drab stripe on the left sleeve for every three years of honorable service.

The tribulations of the early Quartermaster Generals were many, and interesting expedients were resorted to. In February of 1783 was issued from the Newburgh General Headquarters a general order directing all regiments to have their uniforms turned because new cloth had not arrived from abroad. Great care was enjoined to have all uniforms when remade of the same cut and pattern. Perhaps, concluded the order, scarlet cloth may be furnished those regiments of artillery and light infantry using it for facings.

March 3 of the same year provides the following gem: "The regiments (of artillery) which have not turned and repaired their coats are to draw lots of the scarlet cloth which arrived yesterday."

The colors of the various arms and branches then extant were established during the first reorganization after the Revolution. White and blue were generally assigned to the infantry, red to the artillery. To the Quartermaster Corps was given the buff which it still wears and the Inspector General's department was also named.

Even as now there was but one uniform prescribed after the first war. The difference was that it was a dress uniform, civilian clothes being worn for undress occasions, while today the reverse is the case. By 1816 many different sorts of uniforms and equipment were being worn. It was necessary for the War Department to issue an order prohibiting army officers from "wearing dirks in lieu of swords."

Uniform regulations of pre-Civil War days had a more flowery sound than those of the present. As a sort of preamble to those of 1821, the first paragraph reads: "Dark blue is the national color. When a different one is not expressly prescribed, all uniform coats, whether of officers or enlisted men, will be of that color." In that year, "in the interests of economy, comfort and uniformity," the first regulations for an undress uniform were issued. This was to be worn on "such occasions and on such duties as the regulations or customs of the service do not require an officer to be in full dress." In the orders of the same year it was specified that "after the 1st day of January, 1830, citizens' dress shall not be worn by any officer when in camp, on duty or on the march."

From this time forward the variation between the clothe of civilians and the military became increasingly pronounced. The cut of uniform was affected by those of other armies instead of the costumes of the land, and particularly by the uniforms introduced by Frederick the Great.

It is said that Frederick drank. If he did he had a military jag, because he is credited with originating the expression, "solidierly appearance," along with the stock which forced the soldier's chin into the air.

After the 1825 period American uniforms were changed almost from year to year, varying with the vagaries of European styles. After the Civil War the uniforms prescribed were many and varied, becoming more and more sumptuous until about the beginning of this century, when a set of liberal with braid and color but lacking the Victorian prodigality was adopted.

The British Army was the first definitely to sever the field from the dress uniform, and this divergence has remained more complete than in any other forces. Previous to the Crimean campaign soldiers' coats had been becoming tighter and their headdress bulkier and elaborate to the point of what now appears ludicrous. This had gone so far that some cavalry regiments could not do sabre drill in the clothes they were expected to fight in, and the caps of one Hussar regiment in the Crimea were so high and widespreading that the troopers could not execute a downward sword cut at a dismounted enemy. This resulted in a violent reaction, and the sloppier the better became the motto. Large, roomy coats, comfortable headgear and serviceable rather than flashy colors in uniforms were the result. The dress uniforms of the various regiments were retained for peace time parade and ceremony, their value as an aid to morale and discipline being wisely realized.

This action of the British forces had an immediate effect on all European armies and on that of the United States. While the line between dress and field was not so closely drawn here, it existed, and became more pronounced after the Spanish War.

For the first time in many generations the service coat of one army, the British, now conforms to the civilian cut of clothes. Officers of that service wear a coat with lapel collar and vented back. This sacrificed the military and perhaps somewhat of smartness of appearance to comfort, but with the dress, mess, full dress uniforms, &c., which they have in addition to this, it is not of such importance as it would be to the American Army.

Army Will Try Out Would-Be Aviators

SPECIAL TO THE NEW YORK TIMES | SEPT. 14, 1930

WASHINGTON, SEPT. 13, 1930 — A total of 246 students will on Nov. 1 begin an eight months' course of flying training at the two primary flying schools of the Army Air Corps at Brooks Field, San Antonio, Texas, and March Field, Riverside, Cal. Those completing the course successfully will then be transferred to the flying school at Kelly Field, San Antonio, for a four months' advanced course.

Among the new students are eighty-seven second lieutenants of the regular army, who graduated from West Point last June, three officers from other branches of the regular army, 131 candidates from civil life, twenty-four enlisted men from the Army Air Corps and one enlisted man from the infantry.

Brooks Field will begin the training of 124 of these students, comprising three officers of the regular army, forty-one West Point graduates, nineteen enlisted men and sixty-one civilian candidates. The 122 new students due to answer roll-call at March Field comprise forty-six West Point graduates, six enlisted men of the regular army and seventy civilian candidates.

With the reawakening of interest in aviation to an unusual degree during the past several years, the Army Air Corps was able to appoint as flying cadets only a fraction of the number of applicants found eligible for such appointment. For the coming November class the Air Corps had an eligible list of approximately 300 names. With the completion of the new training center at Randolph Field, San Antonio, the Air Corps will be able to accommodate more eligible candidates than is possible at the present time.

California, which has consistently led the other States in the number of native sons sent to the army flying schools, again takes the lead with twenty-two successful candidates, followed by Illinois with sixteen and Texas fifteen.

Draft Board Drama

BY BURTON LINDHEIM | MAY 18, 1941

Behind the numbers of the army lottery are countless human interest stories which the boards must hear.

JOHN JONES has been drafted. It sounds very simple, but back of every draft number called is a human drama, usually relieved by touches of comedy. Most of these dramas are played out in the thousands of draft board offices scattered over the country. Here are some of them.

***

Not only must local draft boards fill their quotas with able-bodied soldiers to be, but they must reject men who should not be in the Army. And sometimes that is quite a job. An indignant medical officer stamped into one local board to ask why they had sent him a man with crossed eyes, a hernia and partial paralysis. The embarrassed chairman explained it was the only way they could get the invalid to leave the board and stop insisting that he be accepted.

***

Many of the men who hurriedly married when the draft law went into effect have decided that martial life is better than marital life after all and are insistent that they be sent immediately to camp. "Dear sir: I marry my man. Later he run away to the Army. Please bring him back." This is a not infrequent letter to the boards.

***

Youngsters far under military age are another problem. "But what," asked one chairman of a youth who was trying to enlist through the board, "will your family say when they hear you are leaving them?" Small fry grinned: "They'll just say 'Good-bye, sucker,' " he said.

***

The boards must reject men who are morally unfit. A minor public enemy appeared before one board to protest his rejection and the chairman showed him a sheet of paper bearing a long list of felony convictions and asked him what about it. The neighborhood Capone dismissed it all with a wave of the hand: "Aw, that's the cops persecutin' me."

***

One young man, rejected because he had to support his mother, brought the mother before the board to testify that he was free to go. "I have been a teacher," she said, "and I can find a job again to support myself." The board stuck to its ruling however and the young man must remain at home — at least until the mother actually has a job.

***

Sometimes the boards help out the young men who want to get into uniform. One board sent a Polish refugee to school and within one month he crammed enough English vocabulary to understand Army commands.

***

At other times the boards' efforts fail to help. A young man, son of a Polish father and an American mother, thought that he was born in the upstate town where he spent his childhood. A neighbor there thought he was born abroad. The board could find no records to give an official status to this man who has become a man without a country. A Scandinavian seaman tried to enlist, but was rejected because he could not take out his first citizenship papers; he had jumped ship and was in the country illegally.

***

Many times the boards must help men get their jobs back after the men, certain that they would be selected, had quit. One young foreign-born registrant quit his job, packed his suitcase and reported to the board with his whole family as soon as he had received his questionnaire. He was immediately put in a deferred classification because he was supporting his mother and two sisters and one of the board members spent a lot of time on the telephone to be sure that he would have his job back next day.

***

Many are the stories the local draft boards hear from those who would not serve. There was a jaunty little man who walked into one draft office to find a buxom woman staring at him. He flinched, then drew himself erect and announced that he claimed her as a dependent. She grimly agreed and showed the board a warrant for his arrest for non-support. The board, acting as a domestic relations court for the moment, offered to grant him a deferment provided he would sign a pledge to support his wife. He did and they went out together.

***

A much-married man who was not contributing to the support of his first two wives and the children he had by them, listed his third wife as a dependent. Summoned to the draft board to corroborate his statement, she said, after a moment's hesitation, "No, he don't support me, neither."

***

A delicate problem in the dance was presented to a board. It finally decided that a ballet dancer who claimed exemption on the grounds that heavy brogans would ruin his finely trained toes would wear the brogans anyway and that a vaudeville dancer who wanted to be drafted would not be — at least until he had completed his bookings — because his girl partner was supporting her mother on income from their act.

***

The personalities of conscientious objectors sometimes appear incongruous to the boards. There was a burly pacifist who pounded the table and roared: "If you don't exempt me I'll go to the appeal board, I'll go to the President himself, I'll fight, fight for my rights."

***

Another conscientious objector saw so much military during the Russian Revolution that he resolved to shun the military forever. He appended twenty typewritten pages to his questionnaire expounding his Tolstoyan views on war and peace. A native-born pacifist requested exemption because he was a convert to Taoism, a Chinese religion.

***

A mother appeared to ask exemption for her son because he could not bear the sight of blood. "Why, the other night," she said, "we saw a movie of the Northwest Mounted Police. There was a scene of violence. My son fainted." "Was it in technicolor?" asked the board chairman.

***

Another mother viewed her son's plea for deferment on the grounds that he was supporting his family in another light, "Please send him to the Army," she urged. "He gamble, he drink, he give nothing at home. He no good."

***

Representatives of all races from the American melting pot come before the draft board. A Negro patriot in his fervor to serve his country ignored the mere detail of filling out his questionnaire. Instead he just scrawled over it, "I ready when you ready." A Harlem musician, however, requested a deferment so he could complete the symphony he was composing. He said he felt he would make a better soldier after he had finished his magnum opus.

***

The members of the bachelor colony in Chinatown, who cannot claim exemption for dependents in China, generally accept the draft with oriental placidity. To many of them the Army means better hours than in a laundry or chop suey house, but to some it means losing a business laboriously built up. A not-so-clever Chinese, reluctant to give up his profitable laundry, told the draft board, "No speakee 'melican." But, unfortunately for himself, he had already answered the questions of the examining physician in good English.

***

Foreign-born citizens regularly display real patriotism. An immigrant who got his first papers months after draft registration day visited a draft board and sought to register, even though he had been informed it was unnecessary. Naturalized citizens burst into patriotic speeches in broken English when volunteering. Over-age refugees endeavor to enlist.

***

One selectee with the minimum of teeth necessary for induction was walking from the draft board, when he overheard some men on the corner make jeering remarks about the selective service. He resented these aspersions, forcibly. A minute later he had two teeth less than the minimum.

***

The misinformation of some persons surprises draft boards. A woman wanted to know if the draft of her husband was grounds for divorce. A truck driver, in filling out the part of his questionnaire relating to dependents, said he was the sole support of an aged truck.

***

Some persons apparently regard the draft board as a philanthropic institution. One New York woman, who had not seen her drafted son in six months, asked the draft board for carfare to visit him. He was stationed in Fort Houston, Texas.

***

Colonel Arthur V. McDermott, director of the selective service in New York City, is impartial. If a favor is asked, the invariable answer is "See your local board."

Army, Navy to Back Work-or-Fight Law for All Men 18 to 45

BY C. P. TRUSSELL | JAN. 9, 1945

WASHINGTON, JAN. 8, 1945 — The full power of the Army, Navy and Selective Service will be thrown behind Administration appeals for immediate enactment of legislation to subject to induction registrants in 4-F classification and all others between the ages of 18 and 45 who do not obtain or remain in essential war jobs.

After conferences of key men dealing with armed service and production manpower problems, held today at the Office of War Mobilization and Reconversion, it was indicated that at hearings starting on Wednesday before the House Committee on Military Affairs united support of the services would be given to the May-Bailey-Brewster Bill.

Under it those inducted could be assigned to special service units and could be put, under military discipline, into essential jobs in war-production plants. While in such units they would not be entitled to mustering-out pay or other regular service benefits.

ONLY BILL TO BE CONSIDERED

This legislation, introduced in the Senate and House on Saturday, after President Roosevelt in his message called for using the services of 4,000,000 4-F's in "whatever capacity is best for the war effort," will be the only measure before the House committee, according to Andrew J. May, coauthor and Military Affairs chairman.

He said, however, that before the measure was sent to the House it might have attached to it proposals for drafting nurses, also requested by the President.

Later, Mr. May said, the committee might turn to consideration of general national legislation, enactment of which the President urged "at the earliest possible moment," but suggested that 4-F controls be dealt with first.

As these preparations for swift action by the House committee were being made, Selective Service officials suggested that employers in essential businesses "would be wise" if they obtained occupational deferments for all employees now classified 4-F in order to keep them on the job.

Though they did not send out any formal notice to employers, a spokesman said that it would be "a natural thing" for them to want to obtain deferments which would tend to "freeze" 4-F's in their production places.

FIRST LADY FOR WIDER ACT

Mrs. Franklin D. Roosevelt said at a news conference that she favored a national service act which would provide for the registration of women as well as men, rather than legislation which would single out nurses for induction.

"Nevertheless, if we must have nurses we have to have them," she added.

"There has been a kind of psychological feeling against doing anything compulsory so far as women are concerned; it will take a great deal of need to do it."

Asserting that "like everything we do, we do so much too late," Mrs. Roosevelt pointed out that needs had been under-estimated and observed that in England where needs were really great, everyone was registered for military services or factory work and put where qualified. This, she said, was "the sensible thing to do."

A combined 4-F control and national service bill, calling for inductions of strikers and willful absentees from war work, was introduced in the House this afternoon by Representative William M. Colmer, Democrat, of Mississippi; chairman of the special committee on post-war economic policy and planning.

His bill would establish a third armed service, the Supply Forces of the United States, which would be charged with the production of articles, commodities and equipment for the prosecution of the war.

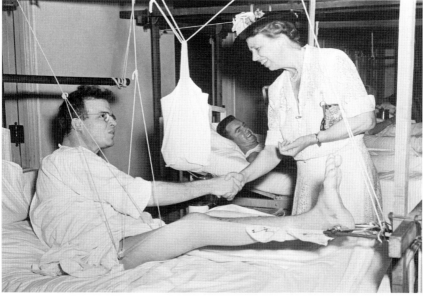

First Lady Eleanor Roosevelt visits with a wounded corporal in March 1944.

Into this third service all draft registrants who had been deferred would be inducted automatically on inactive status, but would be subject to call to active service in war plants or elsewhere when they were found to be contributing to critical manpower shortages.

Those of the Supply Forces would wear a distinctive uniform and when sent into war plants would work at their regular service pay.

Linked with the provisions under which strikers and habitual absentees would be subjected to induction in the third military arm is one under which profits on war production would be limited to 6 per cent on contracts exceeding $10,000.

Mr. Colmer said he would press for early hearings, but Chairman May said that the committee would not consider it in connection with the pending measure.

CRITICISM BY REPUBLICANS

The "penalty" provisions of the May-Bailey-Brewster Bill under went criticism this morning as the Senate Republican Steering Committee discussed this and many other measures at a closed hearing.

Senator Robert A. Taft of Ohio, chairman of the steering body, said later that they were "too severe." Senator Warren R. Austin of Vermont said that if he decided to support such limited national service legislation he probably would seek to eliminate "some of the stigmatizing nature" of the measure.

Mr. Austin, co-author of the Austin-Wadsworth National Service Bill which failed to receive Military Committee approval last year, contended that the May-Baily-Brewster Bill "would not take the place of national service at all."

"It is based upon an erroneous theory of the liability of our citizens," he said, "The American theory, embodied in the Declaration of Independence and the Constitution, is that all citizens are liable to contribute according to their ability to the defense of the nation.

"Its principle appears to be to use 4F's under penalty, not in combat units but in industry. The authority rests wholly in the Selective Service Act which does not contemplate a civilian contribution to the war but a purely military one.

"Penalties of a rather ignominious type are military and tend to reflect on the 4F's to an unfair degree. It is a perversion of the principles of the Selective Service Act.

"I may find it necessary to go along with this bill for a lack of something better, but I may try to remove those parts that put unfair onus on an individual."

He called for "a more active and earnest effort by the Administration" to make it clear that "a broad national service act is needed" and warned that "intermediate legislation may cost lives while we are waiting to get it."

The R.O.T.C. — II: Compulsory Aspect Cause of Argument Within the Services and the Colleges

BY HANSON W. BALDWIN | AUG. 23, 1960

THE COMPULSORY CHARACTER of many Reserve Officers' Training Corps programs is an issue between the services and in the educational field.

The Morrill Act of 1862 required so-called land grant colleges (established by grants of federally controlled public lands), such as Ohio State University, the University of Wisconsin and others to offer courses in military tactics. The 1916 National Defense Act, with its R.O.T.C. program, absorbed the military training program of the land grant colleges. The Morrill Act did not require compulsory attendance of all students at such courses. Nevertheless, a large number of colleges, including a few private ones, and virtually all the land grant and state colleges have required, as a result of action by State Legislatures, Board of Regents or faculty, all students to attend basic R.O.T.C. courses for the first two years of college. The advanced courses in the last two years are voluntary. About 154 of the 248 colleges participating in the Army program require R.O.T.C. for the first two years.

About half of the 175 Air Force R.O.T.C. units are elective; the others are compulsory. The Navy's program is entirely voluntary.

The question of compulsory versus voluntary R.O.T.C. programs has been, at one time or another, an issue on college campuses, but it has become something of a national issue only in recent years. College campuses are divided on the subject; many student bodies are opposed to the compulsory courses as a waste of time. They have had, in many cases, the support of faculty members, and, more recently, of the Air Force and inferentially of the Department of Defense.

ELECTIVE AT 3 SCHOOLS

To date some eighteen colleges and universities — all, except Bucknell and Lehigh, state or land grant institutions — have experienced considerable controversy about the compulsory feature of the program.

In the 1959–60 school year only three out of more than sixty-four land grant colleges and universities had an elective rather than a compulsory R.O.T.C. program. But the list of colleges that have changed from required to elective military science courses has increased since the end of the school year and now includes Ohio State University, the University of Wisconsin, Cornell University, Rutgers and Bucknell (the latter a private institution). The controversy has by no means ended.

The varying positions of students, faculty and armed services contrast sharply. Many students feel compulsory R.O.T.C. is a waste of time. Others dislike military training. Some regard it as a duty.

SEEN AS UNNECESSARY

Within the Pentagon, the differences between the Air Force–Department of Defense position and the Army are also considerable. Col. William C. Lindley recently explained the Air Force position by describing its concept of the Air Force R.O.T.C. as a "precommission education program rather than a reserve training program." He said the Air Force tended toward a "totally voluntary force." Colonel Lindley pointed out that the compulsory feature of the program with its vast enrollment was costly in dollars, manpower and facilities and that, with increased college enrollments, the basic compulsory R.O.T.C. program promised to become larger and larger at a time when officer manpower requirements will be decreasing. The Air Force military requirements, in other words, do not need a compulsory program.

The Defense Department view, as expressed by Assistant Secretary of Defense Charles C. Finucane, also holds that there is no military requirement for a compulsory basic training program. In fact, the increase in college enrollments in the next decade will mean that if compulsory basic R.O.T.C. remains in effect at all institutions that now require it, the total Army R.O.T.C. enrollments will be about 300,000 in 1970, or "178,000 in excess of requirements," he said.

The Army's view as expressed by Secretary of the Army Wilber M. Brucker and others, challenges these estimates, and declares that "without the compulsory feature of the R.O.T.C. program, the Army qualitative and quantitative peacetime annual requirements for 14,000 commissioned officers cannot be met."

"A compulsory basic course provides a far greater base from which to select cadets [who volunteer] for the advanced course," he said.

How the Draft Reshaped America

OPINION | BY AMY J. RUTENBERG | OCT. 6, 2017

"GREETING: YOU ARE HEREBY ordered for induction in the Armed Forces of the United States." In 1967, more than 300,000 American men opened envelopes with this statement inside. Few pieces of mail ever incited the same combination of panic, anticipation and resignation as a draft notice. The words struck terror in the hearts of many recipients. Others found them comforting after years of waiting for the Selective Service System to come calling.

The Vietnam generation came of age with the threat of military service hovering in the background. Although the Selective Service called relatively few men between the end of the Korean War in 1953 and American escalation in Southeast Asia in 1965, the draft had been in almost continuous operation since before the United States joined World War II. During that time Selective Service, under the leadership of Gen. Lewis B. Hershey, faced little public criticism. In fact, Hershey had shaped it into a venerated institution. Although most men may not have wanted to dedicate two years of their life to active military service, draftees generally acquiesced to Uncle Sam's wishes.

After President Lyndon Johnson mobilized ground troops in 1965, draft calls tripled. With each passing year, more men faced conscription to fight a war with whose goals and methods a significant number disagreed. Stories of privileged men finding ways to beat the draft began to circulate.

Newspaper articles with headlines like "Young Men Dream Up Some Ingenious Ways to Avoid the Draft" and "Avoiding the Draft Is Becoming the Favorite Sport Among Youth" horrified Americans who believed military service should be an equal obligation of male citizenship. At least as portrayed by reporters, these men were almost always middle class, with seemingly All-American families.

Critics at the time and since have identified the Selective Service's system of deferments as the main cause of military inequity during the Vietnam War. Although the Department of Defense did not keep records on the socio-economic status or racial identification of service personnel beyond whether they were African-American or not, there's no doubt that men with fewer resources were less likely to obtain deferments than those with more. As a result, they were more likely to be drafted, serve in combat and die in Vietnam. Long Island's war dead, for example, hailed overwhelmingly from working-class backgrounds.

But why? How is it that the Selective Service, which had used deferments during both World Wars and the Korean War, allowed the situation to become so bad that by 1967 fewer than half of Americans polled believed that the draft operated fairly? For this answer, one must look to the goals of Cold War liberals, both Republican and Democrat. The deferment policies that created such havoc during the Vietnam War were the direct outgrowth of Washington's desire to fight Communism at home as well as abroad.

Deferments are a necessary element of any system of selective military service. If a nation does not require all of its citizens to participate in the armed forces, then someone must decide who goes and who stays.

Deferments allow those with skills needed on the home front to exempt themselves from their military obligations because, especially during the upheaval of war, they ensure a viable domestic economy and stable society. Factories, hospitals and schools, for example, can operate only when fully staffed with skilled employees. Farmers and agricultural workers maintain necessary food supplies. In theory, deferments should be limited only to those considered more valuable to war aims as civilians than as soldiers.

But the nature of the Cold War, especially early on, complicated things. Defeating Communism was more than a military endeavor; the home front became a crucial site of defense operations. Americans believed that triumph over the Soviet Union required a prolonged ideological, technological and economic struggle. The circumstances of the

Antiwar demonstrators burn their draft cards on the steps of the Pentagon during the Vietnam War in 1972.

Cold War, therefore, granted the Selective Service System license to use deferments as a tool of social engineering.

Hershey believed that all able-bodied American men had the obligation to serve the nation, but he began to advocate a definition of service that included civilian pursuits, particularly in science, mathematics and engineering. Throughout the 1950s, the perception that the United States was in danger of falling behind the Soviets caused national panic, especially after the U.S.S.R. successfully launched its Sputnik satellite in 1957.

According to politicians and intellectuals, American superiority rested on outpacing Soviet technological development, both in the domestic realm and in the military sector. The Army's strategic plans for countering atomic attack depended on the invention of new weapons, while consumer capitalism required new products to buy and sell. The United States needed a steady supply of men in STEM fields to develop the state-of-the-art appliances and futuristic weapons systems that it so desperately wanted.

In Hershey's view, the Selective Service was the "storekeeper" of America's manpower supply. He believed that the promise of deferments could be used as a tool to coerce — or bribe — men to go to college and enter occupations defined as in the national interest. In the words of one planning memo, the Selective Service could use the "club of induction" to "drive" individuals into "areas of greater importance." This policy, known as manpower channeling, specifically defined these pursuits as service to the state on a par with military service.

The availability of deferments for men attending college and in professional fields ballooned. Occupational deferments increased by 650 percent between 1955 and 1963. But men had to qualify for higher education and be able to pay for it. Since part-time students did not receive deferments, men could not take semesters off to earn tuition money or recover from academic probation. Eligible occupations skewed toward those with college degrees. Unlike during World War II, most factory and agricultural workers could not gain occupational deferments by the late 1950s. Such dispensations were reserved for scientists, engineers, doctors and teachers.

Even those deferments theoretically available to anyone really were not. Medical deferments, for example, were harder for poorer men to obtain. The doctors performing the cursory exams at pre-induction physicals often failed to detect health defects that would have guaranteed exemptions from military service. And if men did not have a record of private medical care, they had little recourse when declared available for service.

By 1965, many middle-class men had come to expect deferments. Military service, to them, was for "suckers" who had made poor choices. Working-class men, of course, were not "suckers." Rather, Great Society policies meant to strengthen the economy by alleviating poverty ended up targeting them for military service.

Policy makers in the Kennedy and Johnson administrations began to focus on America's poor as the weak link between national strength and the promise of democracy. Secretary of Labor W. Willard Wirtz identified the Selective Service as an "incomparable asset" in locating men who could benefit from government aid. Virtually all American men underwent a pre-induction exam. Approximately one-third failed. Such "rejectees" were overwhelmingly from poor and minority backgrounds. In early January 1964, less than two months after taking office, Johnson ordered the Selective Service, the Department of the Army, the Department of Labor and the Department of Health, Education and Welfare to address the problem.

Secretary of Defense Robert McNamara actively wanted the armed forces to be part of the solution. He firmly believed that military service could be used to "rehabilitate" men caught in the cycle of poverty. He, along with Assistant Secretary of Labor Daniel Patrick Moynihan, argued that military training freed poor men from the "squalid ghettos of their external environment" and the "internal and more destructive ghetto of personal disillusionment and despair." McNamara wanted a program that would bolster national security by eliminating a source of social unrest and benefit American combat readiness by boosting the number of men in uniform.

In August 1966, he announced the Defense Department's intention to bring up to 100,000 previously ineligible men into the military each year to "salvage" them. Project 100,000, as it came to be known, would "rescue" poor and especially minority men from the "poverty-encrusted environments" in which they had been raised. These so-called New Standards men — who were otherwise ineligible for military service — were to be admitted into all branches of the armed forces, both voluntarily through enlistment and involuntarily through the draft.

Over all, all branches of service added a combined total of 354,000 New Standards men to their active-duty rosters between 1966 and 1971, when the program ended. Forty percent of these men were black, at a time when the entire military averaged only 9 percent African-American. McNamara hoped that a stint in the military would make New Standards men better husbands, better fathers and better breadwinners, and thus better citizens. Most ended up as infantrymen in Vietnam.

It was no coincidence that those men who already fit the middle-class mold of domestic masculinity — those men who were college students or teachers or scientists — received deferments. Midcentury liberals believed such men did not need the military to lift them up. Meanwhile, every slot filled by a New Standards man was one a middle-class man avoided.

Ultimately, what made sense during the militarized peace of the Cold War did not during a hot war. Many middle-class men did not consider it their responsibility to serve in the military, especially in a war they often categorized as somewhere on the continuum between unnecessary and immoral. Instead, they learned to work a system designed to encourage them to see military service as a personal choice rather than an obligation. Working-class men simply were not offered the same option.

AMY J. RUTENBERG is an assistant professor of history at Iowa State University and the author of the forthcoming book, tentatively "Making Citizen-Civilians: Cold War Military Manpower Policy and the Origins of Vietnam-Era Draft Resistance."

Morale, Allegiance and Drinking: How Military Challenge Coins Evolved and Spread

BY EMILY BAUMGAERTNER | APRIL 11, 2018

WASHINGTON — Scott Pruitt, the administrator of the Environmental Protection Agency, has proposed a redesign of the agency's commemorative coin, an adaptation of longstanding "challenge coins" exchanged among American troops. From a military drinking tradition to civilian government agencies, here is how the coins have evolved and proliferated.

What are challenge coins?

Military commanders often give pocket-size medallions, called challenge coins, to service members as a mark of camaraderie. A commander's unique coin — often copper, bronze or nickel — carries symbols and mottos denoting the unit or office. Coins are usually circular, but also can be pentagons, spades or even dog tags to be worn around the neck.

Throughout their service, military members use the coins to prove their allegiance when challenged. High-ranking officers and retirees often display a collection of coins in their offices alongside uniform patches and ribbons as a symbol of pride.

"In the military, the coins have always been purely about morale and commitment," said Tracy English, a historian at the Air Force's 37th Training Wing at Joint Base San Antonio-Lackland in Texas. "If you walk into a high-ranking service member's office with a big magnet, chances are you will die."

Where did this tradition come from?

Challenge coins were never officially sanctioned, so the history behind the tradition is widely debated among military historians. A common narrative purports that a wealthy American lieutenant in World War I distributed matching bronze coins to his unit members before they were deployed. When an American fighter pilot was captured by Germans and escaped to a French outpost, he was assumed to be a German spy — until he presented the challenge coin around his neck. According to the tale, the coin saved his life — and earned him a bottle of French wine as reparation.

Other historians believe the tradition began in an infantry-run bar in Vietnam, where patrons were required to present enemy bullets or their challenge coin upon entrance.

In keeping with either narrative, challenge coins still earn service members their share of alcohol. Military members often tap their challenge coins upon meeting in a bar — shouting, "Coin check!" — and anyone who either cannot produce one or is the last to show it buys the first round of drinks.

How has it since evolved?

Challenge coin traditions have climbed to the highest ranks of the military. In 2011, Robert M. Gates, then the defense secretary, shook hands with United States troops in Afghanistan, passing duplicates of his challenge coin to each of them as a token of gratitude.

All presidents since Bill Clinton have also carried distinctly designed challenge coins to present to foreign dignitaries and military personnel. President George W. Bush often gave them to injured troops returning from the Middle East; President Barack Obama made a tradition of passing them to service members stationed at the stairs of Air Force One.

But largely because of custom-design coin companies, challenge coins have seeped beyond the military to other government agencies and offices: Secretaries of transportation and agriculture have designed their own coins; so have senators and even local fire departments.

"How and when that jump to civilian life began, we don't exactly know," Mr. English said. "I've seen small companies throughout San Antonio with their own coins. I recently got one from a Boy Scout."

Some consider the proliferation a symbol of solidarity with the American military. Others see it as the contorting of an honored ritual

President Barack Obama giving a presidential challenge coin at Marine Corps Air Station Miramar in California in 2014.

for bragging rights in Washington, collecting the coins as weighty business cards or displaying them as autographs.

Who funds the coins?

Challenge coins can cost $5 to $10 each, so agencies can spend thousands of dollars on the tokens each year. In some areas of government, leaders are said to purchase the coins out of their own personal accounts.

In the military, some units have booster clubs that generate money for challenge coins. Other commanders are authorized to purchase "morale boosters" with government funds, Mr. English said. The Department of Defense did not respond to a request for comment on challenge coin funding.

"If you buy a whole bunch coins and a new Mercedes, maybe that's a problem," Mr. English said. "Otherwise, folks are often supportive of keeping with the tradition."

Navy Returns to Compasses and Pencils to Help Avoid Collisions at Sea

BY ERIC SCHMITT | SEPT. 27, 2017

WASHINGTON — Urgent new orders went out earlier this month for United States Navy warships that have been plagued by deadly mishaps this year. More sleep and no more 100-hour workweeks for sailors. Ships steaming in crowded waters like those near Singapore and Tokyo will now broadcast their positions as do other vessels. And ships whose crews lack basic seamanship certification will probably stay in port until the problems are fixed.

All seemingly obvious standards, military officials say, except that the Navy only now is rushing the remedies into effect after two collisions in two months left 17 sailors dead, despite repeated warnings about the looming problems from congressional watchdogs and the Navy's own experts dating to 2010.

"Many of the issues we're discussing today have been known to Navy leaders for years. How do we explain that, Admiral?" Senator John McCain of Arizona, the Republican chairman of the Armed Services Committee, demanded of Adm. John Richardson, the chief of naval operations, at a hearing last week.

"Senator, there is no explanation," Admiral Richardson said.

The orders issued recently by the Navy's top officer for ships worldwide, Vice Adm. Thomas S. Rowden, drew on the lessons that commanders gleaned from a 24-hour fleetwide suspension of operations last month to examine basic seamanship, teamwork and other fundamental safety and operational standards.

Collectively, current and former officers said, the new rules mark several significant cultural shifts for the Navy's tradition-bound fleets. At least for the moment, safety and maintenance are on par with operational security, and commanders are requiring sailors to use old-fashioned compasses, pencils and paper to help track potential hazards, as well as reducing a captain's discretion to define what rules the watch team follows if the captain is not on the ship's bridge.

"Rowden is stomping his foot and saying, 'We've got to get back to basics,' " said Vice Adm. William Douglas Crowder, a retired commander of the Seventh Fleet and a former deputy chief of naval operations, who reviewed the four-page directive issued on Sept. 15, a copy of which was obtained by The New York Times. "We ought to be doing this anyhow."

Admiral Richardson is expected to announce additional guidance to the Navy in the next several days that builds off Admiral Rowden's directive. "We took some time to stop, take a break and review our fundamentals, to ensure that we're operating safely and effectively and to correct any areas that required immediate attention," Admiral Richardson told the senators last week.

The new orders come as the fallout continues from four Navy accidents in the western Pacific this year, including the two fatal crashes: the destroyer Fitzgerald colliding with a freighter near Tokyo in June, and a second destroyer, the John S. McCain, colliding with a tanker last month while approaching Singapore.

The commander of the Navy's Pacific Fleet, Adm. Scott H. Swift, said this week that he would retire after being notified that he was no longer in the running to take charge of the Pentagon's overall Pacific Command, which would oversee any military operations against North Korea.

Vice Adm. Joseph P. Aucoin, the former head of the Seventh Fleet, based in Japan and the Navy's largest overseas, was removed last month in connection with the accidents. And Admiral Rowden himself has also said he will retire early.

It has been a sobering time for commanders not just in the Seventh Fleet, which has been closely scrutinized, but also the Navy's other fleets based overseas. They are all taking a hard look at how to balance their operational requirements against eroding training and maintenance standards.

"We found some things about risk that didn't match what we thought, and we're making changes in things we discovered," Vice Adm. Kevin M. Donegan, commander of the Fifth Fleet based in Bahrain, said in a telephone interview.

"When we have something like this happen, we do rigorous homework," Admiral Donegan said. "We're not standing fast."

There is little argument, however, that a shrinking Navy is performing the same duties that a larger fleet did a decade ago, and that constant deployments leave little time to train and maintain ships amid their relentless duties.

Gen. Joseph F. Dunford Jr., the chairman of the Joint Chiefs of Staff, told senators during a hearing on Tuesday about his visit to the Navy destroyer Barry several months ago, and of his learning that the ship had been at sea for 70 percent of the past 12 months.

"When we go back now and we look at were they able to do all the training necessary, and what was their life like during those 12 months, 70 percent of the time underway is an unsustainable rate," General Dunford said. "We're going to have to make adjustments in the demand. That will incur managing operational and strategic risk, there's no doubt."

Many of the changes in Admiral Rowden's order smack of simple common sense. Hard to see and track electronically, naval vessels have long posed special perils to nighttime navigation. In addition to radar, all but the smallest commercial vessels use the so-called Automatic Identification Systems to broadcast information about their position, course and speed. Military vessels typically carry the systems but often turn them off because the captains do not want to reveal so much information. That will change under the new orders.

"Successful mission accomplishment cannot be our sole measure of effectiveness," Admiral Rowden said in his directive. "We must take greater heed of the manning, maintenance, training and certification pillars that collectively foster success."

Admiral Rowden also ordered standardized rules for watch teams on the bridge when the captain is not present; new reporting requirements for major equipment failures and near misses; and manually tracking vessels that come with 5,000 yards of a Navy ship to avoid collisions.

The Navy has allowed ships to rely on grueling watch schedules that leave captains and crews exhausted, even though the service ordered submarines to abandon similar schedules two years ago. A Government Accountability Office report from May said sailors were on duty up to 108 hours each week.

The new rules essentially will adopt studies by the Naval Postgraduate School to develop a shorter watch schedule to match circadian rhythms, which uses three hours of watch duty and nine hours off. Recognizing the benefits, the Navy ordered submarines to move to a similar schedule in 2015.

Senators harrumphed last week that sleep-deprived sailors presented an obvious problem begging for a solution. "If we know that somebody's working a 100-hour workweek, I'm not sure we need a study," Mr. McCain said acidly.

A World War II Mystery Is Solved, and Emotions Flood In

BY MIKE IVES | MAY 28, 2018

AFTER THE B-24 BOMBER carrying Second Lt. Thomas V. Kelly Jr. was shot down off the coast of what is now Papua New Guinea in 1944, his parents had a gray tombstone etched with a drawing of the plane and the words "In Loving Memory."

The 21-year-old bombardier's remains were never recovered, and for years, his relatives rarely discussed the pain they felt over his death.

"There were Christmas songs that would come on that my mom couldn't even listen to," said Diane Christie, Lieutenant Kelly's niece.

But in 2013, one of Ms. Christie's second cousins found a website with information about the bomber he had been on. That led to years of archival research, culminating in a recent search of the ocean floor by a team of oceanographers and archaeologists.

A few weeks ago, Ms. Christie's phone rang as she was shopping for groceries in Folsom, Calif. Her sister was calling to say that Lieutenant Kelly's plane — nicknamed Heaven Can Wait — had been found.

"I literally walked outside Whole Foods, and I burst into tears," Ms. Christie said. "And I'm like, where did this come from? I didn't even know my uncle."

Heaven Can Wait is one of 30 United States aircraft retrieved by Project Recover, a six-year-old nonprofit that collaborates with the Defense POW/MIA Accounting Agency, or D.P.A.A., the arm of the Pentagon tasked with finding and returning fallen military personnel.

The group says its recoveries show how new sonar and robotics technologies make it far easier to find planes that crashed at sea, and that were once thought lost for good.

"It really opens up the possibility that more families can learn what happened to their family members who have been missing all this

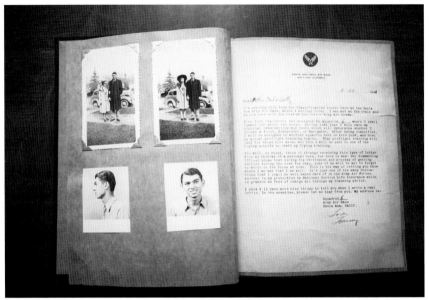

A family scrapbook showing pictures of Lieutenant Kelly with, top left, his mother, Theresa M. Kelly; and top right, his sister, Betty Kelly. At right is a letter he sent his family.

time," said Patrick Scannon, the president of the BentProp Project, a California-based nonprofit that cooperated on the effort to find the B-24.

Since 1973, the Pentagon has recovered the remains of 2,381 United States service members and civilians, according to the military's data. Of the more than 72,000 American service members from World War II who are still unaccounted for, approximately 26,000 are considered possibly recoverable.

The Pentagon says the number of missing United States service members identified worldwide has been rising in recent years, thanks largely to advancements in forensic science.

But as time passes, identifying remains grows harder, and it becomes more difficult to find surviving family members who can provide DNA samples, said Sgt. First Class Kristen Duus, a spokeswoman for D.P.A.A. in Washington.

"Time's not necessarily on our side," she said.

Before searching for missing aircraft, the Project Recover team tries to pinpoint the crash locations by interviewing veterans and analyzing historical records and modern satellite imagery. Then it searches with tools that can include thermal cameras and a sonar-equipped robot that looks like a torpedo and swims just above the seafloor.

The recovery and identification of remains from these underwater sites are conducted at the Pentagon's discretion. Of the 30 aircraft that Project Recover has found so far, 27 are associated with 113 missing service members, and the remains of five airmen have been repatriated.

The Heaven Can Wait bomber was found last year in Hansa Bay, on Papua New Guinea's northern coast, where five United States aircraft are believed to have gone down during World War II.

Lieutenant Kelly's bombing mission on March 11, 1944, was part of an American effort to disrupt Japanese shipping and supply chains ahead of attacks that spring on a Japanese airfield nearby and another 360 miles northwest, said Michael J. Claringbould, a historian in Australia who specializes in World War II-era aviation in the Pacific. Many Japanese military personnel would eventually flee into nearby jungles and die of starvation.

Much of the research that helped the Project Recover team pinpoint the bomber's location in Hansa Bay was conducted over several years by a team of family members led by Ms. Christie's second cousin Scott L. Althaus.

Mr. Althaus, a professor of political science at the University of Illinois Urbana-Champaign, said his project began on Memorial Day five years ago with an online search for information about Lieutenant Kelly. "It snowballed from there," he said.

He later sent Ms. Christie and three other family members to the World War II archives at the University of Memphis, where they photographed more than 800 documents associated with the plane and its crew from the U.S. Army Air Force. (The U.S. Air Force was not established until 1947.)

He also spoke by phone with a scuba diver in Belgium who had once lived near Hansa Bay and offered guesses about where the bomber might have crashed. Mr. Althaus said the point was never to find the plane, but simply to honor Lieutenant Kelly and the other 10 men who had been in it. "Each has a family and a future that they didn't get to inhabit," he said.

The bomber was found in Hansa Bay last October, the year after Mr. Althaus's aunt contacted Project Recover.

Using Mr. Althaus's research as a guide, the team's scientists found the plane's debris field after 11 days searching about 10 square miles of the bay's seafloor with scanning sonars and underwater robots. Project Recover would not comment on the cost of the mission, although Dr. Scannon said that large ones typically cost $200,000 to $400,000.

The Pentagon has not yet decided whether it will try to recover and identify the 11 crew members of Heaven Can Wait, Lt. Col. Kenneth L. Hoffman, a D.P.A.A. spokesman in Hawaii, said in an email. He added that selecting a site for excavation could take months or even years.

Ms. Christie, 61, said by telephone that receiving Lieutenant Kelly's remains would provide even more closure for her family. She has now read all of the letters he wrote home during the war, she said, and his grave in Livermore, Calif., has recently taken on new significance for her.

To honor Lieutenant Kelly and the other crew members, a B-24 bomber flew over the cemetery three times on Sunday. A 21-gun salute and flag-presentation ceremony were also held.

"It was wonderful," Ms. Christie said.

In his correspondence, the young bombardier's tone is often optimistic, even as he acknowledges the hardships and dangers of his assignment. In one letter, he digresses to say he took a break from writing to eat a quart of ice cream.

Ms. Christie said she was struck by how very young her uncle had been, and by his constant concern for how his family was dealing with his absence.

"If we are lucky we might get home by next Christmas, but it's hard to say for sure," Lieutenant Kelly wrote on Feb. 1, 1944, shortly after his 21st birthday.

"How are Mom and Dad?" he wrote on Feb. 29, less than two weeks before he died aboard Heaven Can Wait. "Are they doing a lot of needless worrying?"

CHAPTER 2

Expanding Directives and Personnel

In the late 20th and early 21st century, the branches of military service have faced many new obstacles and issues. They have had to enforce socially progressive directives for the benefit of increasingly diverse military personnel, create strategies to help immigrants become successful U.S. soldiers, remedy declining interest in enlistment and confront a range of terrorist groups and incidents. As the U.S. military has worked to adapt to these changes, they have also faced scrutiny for outdated policies and for how they conduct investigations into crimes committed by personnel.

Pentagon Widens Rules to Prevent Racial Inequities

BY DANA ADAMS SCHMIDT | DEC. 18, 1970

WASHINGTON, DEC. 17 — The Defense Department issued tough directives today to enforce racial equality in the armed forces after it had received a report detailing "frustration and anger" among black troops in West Germany.

The most important effect of the directives may be in the United States because they give base commanders the power to declare housing off limits if landlords practice racial discrimination.

Until now the exercise of such powers by base commanders has required Pentagon authorization, which has rarely been requested. Judge L. Howard Bennett, director of the Pentagon's Equal Opportunity Office, said he could recall only four to six instances in the last three years in which a base commander went to the trouble' of obtaining permission to declare a place off limits for racial reasons.

LIMITED TO THE U.S.

The directives were issued by the Assistant Secretary for Manpower, Roger T. Kelley, after Frank W. Render 2d, Deputy Assistant Secretary for Equal Opportunity, had presented the results of a three-and-a-half week survey of six Army bases in Germany, naval stations in Spain and Italy and Air Force bases' in Britain and Germany.

Mr. Kelley explained that because of delicate problems abroad, the powers given to base commanders applied only to the United States.

The directives summarize and strengthen Pentagon orders. New aspects included call for "numerical goals and timetables as a means to increase utilization of minorities in occupations" where their representation is now out of balance and the removal or reassignment of officers, noncommissioned officers and civilians who refrain from positive action against discrimination.

TURNABOUT IS 'IMPERATIVE'

Defense Department contractors must comply with equal opportunity principles if they expect to continue to do business with the department, according to the directives.

In the introduction to his report, the thrust of which has already become public knowledge, Mr. Render asserted that "a dramatic turnabout of behavior and attitudes in the area of race and human relations is imperative in the military services if we are to maintain highly effective combat and support-oriented units."

But he said in response to questions at a news conference that he did not believe the combat readiness of American troops in West

Germany had been lowered by racial tensions. He added that he felt that the visit by his 15-man mission had calmed black troops there and headed off "violent action."

"We did not anticipate finding such acute frustration and such volatile anger as we found among the blacks, nor did we expect to find a somewhat lower level of frustration which was clearly evidenced by young whites," the report said, referring to attempts to disrupt meetings.

The mission asserted that small groups of alienated blacks at Karlsruhe and Mannheim angrily informed it that they had no reason to be fighting in a white man's army and a white man's war and that "their place was back in the States: New York, Chicago, Atlanta, Detroit, Jacksonville, where they could fight to liberate and free their black sisters and brothers from the dirty, stinky, teeming ghettos and from all forms of racial bigotry and oppression."

Some of the Karlsruhe and Mannheim blacks said they wanted guns, ammunition and grenades because "whitey" understood no approach but violent confrontation. They accused the mission of intending to brainwash them.

Mr. Render said in reply to a question that he had no evidence that the Black Panthers were active among the troops.

The report also made points:

• Most of the commands visited exhibited "an apprehensive, less than positive attitude" toward the mission's purposes.

• While high-ranking officers proved understanding almost everywhere, junior officers and noncommissioned officers and, in some cases, majors and lieutenant colonels seemed unable to communicate the approved racial policies.

• The mission found evidence of discrimination in military justice, the military police, promotions, work assignments and the management of clubs.

The mission, finding housing near military bases in West Germany a subject of special concern, recommended that there be an "equal-opportunity or human-relations officer and a human-relations council" at major units.

It also asked for "mechanisms" to insure effective communication of approved policies through the chain of command, but it did not explain what the mechanisms might be. A "full scale program in education and race relations" should be initiated for the benefit of military personnel at all levels, it said.

Recruiters' New Obstacle: War Fear

BY DAVID GONZALEZ | DEC. 10, 1990

THE NAVY'S RECRUITER of the Year finds his skills being put to the test as he tries to enlist recruits who fear they may be shipped off to the Middle East and to war.

"If you join up, how do you know if you're coming back?" said Daniel Freeman, 17 years old, a junior at Aviation High School in Long Island City, who stood in a knot of students who listened to the recruiter, Petty Officer 1st Class Willie Barnhill.

"I can't speak for the other branches, but you're better off in the Navy," Petty Officer Barnhill replied. "You can take hot showers, watch TV, and we got stuff like toilet tissue and you can go to class."

But what about war?

"Think of the last time a Navy vessel was sunk," he countered during his visit last Friday. "Navy ships are built today not to sink."

Nevertheless, a Navy spokesman said enlistment figures dropped this autumn by as much as 15 percent. The Army has seen an even bigger decline in new recruits, as much as 28 percent in some parts of the country. Military officials said there was no clear trend nationwide, pointing out that the Marine Corps and Air Force have had no decline in enlistments.

Despite the decline, however, none of the branches has failed to meet its goals for people entering to begin basic training, said Christopher Jehn, an Assistant Secretary of Defense for Force Management and Personnel. That is because there is a lag of as much to one year between enlisting and reporting to boot camp.

He said the services have been able to meet current staffing needs by drawing on enlistees who signed up before the Persian Gulf crisis began.

The Army, which is the largest of the military branches, has seen the worst dropoff in new enlistments since the buildup began. It was able to meet 82 percent of October's goal of 10,039 recruits and only 77 percent of November's goal of 7,128, Mr. Jehn said.

Recruiting goals for the Navy have seen a similar but smaller decline, said Petty Officer David Melancon, a Navy spokesman. New enlistments declined to 94 percent of September's goal, 88 percent in October and an estimated 85 percent for November.

"We have to acknowledge the existence" of the buildup in the gulf, said Mr. Jehn. "Kids and their parents are taking a wait-and-see attitude."

The benefits package sounded good to Jason Pugh and two of his friends from Aviation High School when they first visited a Navy recruiting station in Queens last summer — two months before the Iraqi invasion of Kuwait. Now he and his friends are concerned.

"In the back of your mind is: Are they going to send you over there if war broke out?" said Mr. Pugh, a 17-year-old senior. He said his friends are not very interested in the Navy any more.

Autumn has always been a tough season for recruiters, since many young people have yet to decide whether to attend college, look for work or join the military. It has become more difficult because of a shrinking pool of 17-to-21-year-olds and spending cutbacks that reduced the recruiting budget by 15 percent, Mr. Jehn said.

Army recruiters in Atlanta said there has been no shortage of new enlistees and they have exceeded their recruiting goals each month, said Capt. Richard Carroll, operations officer for the Atlanta recruiting battalion.

Some recruiters said they have heard from ex-servicemen about re-enlistment. "They were in the service and didn't see anything or do anything and now this world event is happening and they want to tell their kids they did this," said Staff Sgt. Ron Turner, a Marine recruiter in Seattle.

But at an Army recruiting station in St. Louis, a chart with minus signs next to the names of onetime recruits who decided not to enter the service reminded Sgt. First Class Newarner Coleman Jr. of the effects of the gulf crisis. He has already had two high school seniors and a former serviceman who had re-enlisted pull out at the last minute. Another young man decided to go to college on the day he was supposed to leave for basic training.

Although his station recruited nine people in October — one more than was expected — Sergeant Coleman said not one person enlisted last month.

"Nobody wants to go to war," Sergeant Coleman said. "I joined the Army to get an education."

Yet across town, the Marine Corps recruiting station had its best November in seven years, accomplishing 110 percent of its "mission" last month.

Military officials said none of the services intended to relax entry standards, since recruits must fit into an increasingly high-tech military.

But as an inducement, the military has expanded to 47 the number of hard-to-fill job categories that qualify new recruits for $2,000 sign-up bonuses.

Recruiting pitches that in peacetime were heavy on skills training and education benefits now include discussion of the Middle East crisis and the role of the military.

"We talk about how freedom is not free," said Sgt. 1st Class Lemorris Grover, an Army recruiter in North Seattle, Wash. "You have to pay for it sometimes, and maybe this is one of those times."

But appeals to patriotism are tempered with assurances that it could be more than one year before new recruits finish boot camp and specialized skills training. Furthermore, they are told that not all soldiers are sent into combat.

In Qatar, Forgotten U.S. Warriors Wait

BY JUDITH MILLER | DEC. 25, 1990

THEY ARE THE forgotten 1,000.

There have been no nightly news photos of these members of the United States armed forces, and no television interviews about their mission, living conditions and morale. Unlike the Americans in Saudi Arabia, who have been the focus of lavish attention, these men and women have had virtually no visitors from the states.

Few Americans even know they are here in Qatar, or even where exactly Qatar is. Neither did their commander, Col. Jerry Nelson, who was ordered to bring his F-16's here from the unit's home base at Torrejon, Spain, at the end of August with less than a day's notice.

"I grabbed my National Geographic and looked it up myself to figure out where we were going," Col. Nelson said.

For the past four months, the 48 women and some 900 men of the 401st Tactical Fighter Wing have been sleeping in air-conditioned tents on the national air base in this country, a peninsula the size of Connecticut in the middle of the gulf with an estimated population of roughly 350,000, less than 90,000 of whom are of Qatari descent.

SHARING THOUGHTS OF CHRISTMAS

On Sunday night and this morning, men and women from the 401st shared their thoughts on this Christmas season, the unease fostered by waiting for war and the boredom of their lives here with a small group of American reporters, the first permitted to visit the forces in Doha.

Qatar, among the poorest of the enormously wealthy gulf states and the one with the smallest population, did not hide the American presence here. But it did not exactly boast about it either. Although Qatar is not a likely military target, neither Qatar nor any of the other gulf sheikdoms seems eager to publicize any role as host to the

American military, or the presence of some 550 Canadian pilots and support staff and some 60 members of the French Air Force.

"Qatar never rejected any request to come here," said John Berry, the United States Information Service officer in Doha. "But this is a place that tends to get overlooked. Reporters weren't exactly flocking here."

It was only because of the summit of the Gulf Cooperation Council, the six-member economic and military cooperation group, that the 401st's anonymity ended.

On Sunday night at a Christmas party, Ambassador Mark Hambley, wearing a T-shirt saying "Visit Iraq before Iraq visits you," gave some members of the air wing what they described as "the world's largest postcard" — a 37-pound, 575-foot-long scroll of season's greetings signed by some 10,000 people from Odessa County in Texas. Air wing members sent a collective Christmas cheer back home to friends and family, courtesy of the Cable News Network.

"Americans may not know exactly where we are, but we're getting 8,000 to 9,000 letters a day addressed to 'any soldier,' " said Lieut. Col. Bruce Wright. And then there are the cookies. Some 1,200 pounds of them arrived from the United States the other day. "There is no sugar left in the United States," Col. Nelson said. "We need dentists."

BURGERS CLOSE TO THE BASE

Members of the 401st have tried to get into the Christmas spirit. Some of the 70 tents at what is now called "Doha Air Base Tent City" are decorated with Christmas wreaths and trees. Church services will be held at the tent city tonight and on Christmas Day.

The base has a few comforts of home — a Hardee's fast food stand just outside the American part of the base, a PX with sundries and toiletries and a "morale, welfare, and recreation" tent that has weight-lifting, volleyball and other sports equipment.

Because most of the wing's members are confined to the base most of the time, a Pizza Hut in Doha does a landslide take-out business.

But Qatar, like almost all of the Islamic gulf region, does not permit alcohol, so "you can forget about the beer and egg nog," one young airman complained.

"It's really boring," said another airman, Phillip Wallace of Long Island City, Queens. "I just want to get this over with and go home."

'150 PERCENT READY' BY JAN. 15

Several wing members said they looked forward to the Jan. 15 deadline set by the United Nations Security Council for Iraqi forces to leave Kuwait.

Ricardo Febles, a 30-year-old technical sergeant and weapons specialist from Ponce, P.R., said the deadline put a limit on the waiting. "Now the adrenalin is up," he said. "By Jan. 15, we'll be 150 percent ready and raring to go. We'll be sending Saddam a couple of Christmas gifts if he doesn't get his act together."

Homesickness was particularly acute because of Christmas. Sergeant Febles, for example, got married only a month before coming here. "I brought my camera so that when people ask me where I spent my honeymoon, I'll say I spent it in Qatar," he said.

MAINTAINING A RELATIONSHIP

Love has also bloomed here among the thoughts of war in Tent City. Staff Sgt. Cameron Miller, 29, a Sandy, Utah, resident who is in aircraft maintenance, proposed to his superior officer, Technical Sgt. Mary Sousa, from Stoughton, Mass., soon after they came here. She said yes.

"But it's tough because we have to sleep in separate tents," Sergeant Miller said. "All we can do is hold hands, and we can't even do that in town."

Sergeant Sousa added, "We want to get married in April — if it's over by then."

Seeking a Future in Military, Undeterred by Talk of War

BY JOHN W. FOUNTAIN | SEPT. 22, 2001

CHICAGO, SEPT. 21 — There is no hard sell here.

Sandwiched between the Dollar Store and Chop Suey Express in a neon-lighted strip mall on the city's Southwest Side, the red "U.S. Marines" sign is no more distinct than the dozen or so other fluorescent marquees.

It is 11:30 a.m., and business as usual. Inside, Sgt. Leon Shivers, who runs the recruiting station, is a living, breathing billboard, dressed in his wrinkle-less Marine blue slacks, tan shirt and spit-shined shoes.

Jose Pereida, 17, strolls in on his lunch break from nearby Curie High School. He has been stopping in for months now. A senior, Mr. Pereida, like many other inner-city youths, is strapped for cash, short on options. He said he saw joining the military as a way to pay for college, if not the way to get a jump on a career, to get off the streets, maybe even to find himself.

"They want to just make the best out of you. I like that," Mr. Pereida said. But what of the talk of war since the terrorist attacks on Sept. 11?

"It doesn't change my mind," the gangly Mr. Pereida said.

"I am concerned what can happen if I go to war," added Mr. Pereida, who next spring intends to sign up, war or not, "because my country needs me now more than ever."

Even as thousands of troops head overseas, joining the armed forces remains high on the list for some young people in poor and working-class neighborhoods where enlisting is still seen as a way up, if not out.

Like most other recruiters around the country, Sergeant Shivers said he had seen more people walk through his doors since the terrorist attacks. They still are not lining the sidewalk on South Pulaski

Road, though. And, like elsewhere in the country, actual enlistment has not gone up or down.

The talk of war swirling around the country is a concern, potential recruits here say, but apparently not enough to scare them away here.

Some come from neighborhoods like Bridgeport, a hardscrabble blue-collar community to the east and the LeClaire Courts housing projects to the west, and even from the city's West Side, where pitfalls sometimes seem as plenteous as potholes. The military can look just great to a poor city kid in peacetime.

But how about when the drums of war are pounding in the wind?

The way Pablo Moran sees it, the armed forces provide a stable job and benefits. Mr. Moran, 18, recently completed Marine Corps basic training and returned this week to the Pulaski recruiting station where he had enlisted. But this time he was there to accompany a recruiter to his high school as living proof of the transforming power of the corps. Recently married, he and his wife are expecting a child soon. Mr. Moran has no regrets, even now.

"I had no plans after school. I was just one of those students that just wanted to graduate," said Mr. Moran, a smiley young man with a fresh crew cut.

When his friends saw him at school this week, they said, " 'Hey man, you're walking straight now,' " he said, laughing.

Mr. Moran's former school friends also had something else to say in light of the military buildup in the Middle East: They said, " 'Oh yeah, you're going to go die over there,' " he recalled.

"But I was going to die over here, too," Mr. Moran said. "So it doesn't really matter. As a teenager, it's more of a risk to be in the streets."

But some not-so-traditional candidates have shown up. Among them an 87-year-old former marine who wanted to re-enlist.

"We said, we thank him for his interest, but unfortunately we couldn't use him," Sergeant Shivers recalled.

That does not mean that the Marines are not still looking for a few good men.

Less than a block from the recruiting station, where scores of young brown, black and white faces, who have enlisted over the years, hang in picture frames on the walls, the Curie High School football team practiced. Their blue or red jerseys were ruffled by the breeze. Many of Coach Louis Acevedo's players will be moving on soon.

His advice: "I tell our kids this: If they want to go into the military, that's fine. But go in the military as an officer," Mr. Acevedo said. "Go to college, and if college isn't for you, then the military is an option."

For players like Benjamin Vargas, 17, and his younger brother, Erick, 16, the military is the best option of financing college without a football scholarship, something that neither is counting on, the brothers say. They live with an aunt. Their father died of diabetes a year ago. Their mother was murdered five years ago. In addition to classes at Curie and playing football, they work part time.

"We help out with the rent, the food, whatever we can," Benjamin Vargas said.

Both brothers are strongly considering the Army for simple reasons.

"Benefits, man," Benjamin Vargas explained. "All I got is myself to take care of me."

He admits he is afraid of the possibility of war "a little bit," but not enough to keep him from enlisting, he said. "If I have to go, I have no choice, I go. You know what I'm saying?"

He trotted off to join his teammates, holding his white helmet, almost completely sold on the military, no hard sell needed, only the facts of life.

Not Yet Citizens but Eager to Fight for the U.S.

BY DAVID W. CHEN AND SOMINI SENGUPTA | OCT. 26, 2001

AS A YOUTH in Kazakhstan, Alexandr Manin had no interest in the war that the Soviet Union was waging in Afghanistan in the 1980's. But since arriving in New York three years ago, he has had a change of heart, and has joined the military.

The United States military, that is.

Mr. Manin, who is here as a legal permanent resident but is not yet a United States citizen, is scheduled to leave on Nov. 5 for basic training with the Marines. The law allows permanent residents like him — those who have a green card — to enlist.

"It doesn't matter that America is not my country; New York is my city, and what happened shook my life," said Mr. Manin, a fast-talking 25-year-old from Greenpoint, Brooklyn. "I feel patriotic, and I have this itch now to go sooner."

Particularly in New York, with its huge population of immigrants, many residents for years have been signing up to fight under the American flag, even though they do not carry an American passport. In fact, immigrant men and women seem more likely to enlist than their native-born peers.

In New York City, 13 percent of those under the age of 18 are immigrants, both legal and illegal. But in the Navy, 1,200, or 40 percent, of all New York City recruits were green-card holders in the last year. In the Marines, the number is 363, or 36 percent; in the Army, it is 589, or 27 percent.

On a national level, the percentage of green-card military recruits is relatively small, hovering around 5 percent for most services. Even so, the proportions have been steadily rising in recent years, especially in cities like Los Angeles and Miami.

There is no simple explanation for why these permanent residents opt for the military. Some do it because they want to speed up the citizenship process. Some do it because they are, like many immigrants, of meager means and believe that the military offers economic and social mobility. And some do it because they feel patriotic and want badly to belong.

That has been especially true during wartime historically, and the weeks after Sept. 11 are no exception.

"There's an us versus them thing," said Philip Kasinitz, a sociologist at Hunter College who studies the assimilation of the children of immigrants. "This happens in wartime generally. As a result, a lot of immigrants and certainly the children of immigrants feel a need to assert which side of the line they are on."

Many of the green-card recruits in New York reflect the city's changing demographics, and come from countries in Latin America and the Caribbean such as the Dominican Republic, Jamaica and Ecuador.

And while there are proportionally fewer recruits with Asian backgrounds, one immigrant from Hong Kong, Wai Wan, a 22-year-old from Sheepshead Bay, Brooklyn, recently joined the Air Force because he thought the technical training would look impressive on his resume. But after Sept. 11, he felt a patriotic tug, too.

"We asked for computer-related jobs," said Mr. Wan, who signed up with a friend, Alex Wong (a Brazilian green card holder). "But now, we've been looking for combat-related jobs."

For immigrants, the military has long served as a gateway to the American mainstream and a ticket to American acceptance. Indeed, to prove their loyalty, many Japanese-American men volunteered in the Second World War, even as their families were forced into internment camps as "enemy aliens."

There are tangible benefits as well. For permanent residents, military service can shorten the wait to apply for citizenship from five to three years.

Between 1994 and 1999, more than 3,600 immigrants became United States citizens through this provision, according to the Immigration and Naturalization Service. There is nothing in immigration law that prohibits illegal immigrants from serving in the military, but the services say anyone without the proper documentation is automatically rejected.

But even those immigrants who do qualify but are not citizens face restrictions, too. They are not eligible for up to $17,000 in college tuition aid under the R.O.T.C. program. They are generally not allowed to perform certain duties, including reconnaissance, intelligence and data systems.

If they are from what the military deems to be a hostile country like Afghanistan or Iraq, they need to go through additional security checks. But residents from Egypt or Saudi Arabia, the birthplace of the Sept. 11 hijackers, are not considered to be from hostile countries and need no special security clearance.

Through the years, a few improbable figures have emerged from the gallery of immigrant soldiers. The Marines can claim the famous — Shaggy, the Jamaican-born and Brooklyn-raised singer — and the infamous — Hussein Mohammed Farah, the son of the late Somali warlord, Gen. Mohammed Farah Aidid.

But the numbers in New York now are stark. In some neighborhoods, like Flatbush in Brooklyn or Washington Heights in Manhattan, up to 90 percent of recruits are not yet citizens.

Some 40 percent of all Naval recruits in New York City in the last fiscal year which ended in September, were green-card holders, up from perhaps 20 percent a decade ago, said Senior Chief Tim Stewart of the Navy Recruiting District New York. Throughout the country, the figure was 8 percent, up from 5 percent in 1995.

The Navy's national recruiter of the year was Petty Officer Second Class Lenny Ramos, whose territory includes most of Manhattan. And one of his most recent green-card recruits was Samantha Ruiz, 19, who moved to Washington Heights 11 years ago from the Dominican Republic and signed up two weeks ago.

This summer, she gave some thought, though not serious, to joining the military because of the citizenship and travel perks. But then came the terrorist attacks.

"That pushed me along to make me really want to join," said Ms. Ruiz, who now spends much of her time as a volunteer in the Navy's recruiting office in Harlem. "This is my home now. And I just felt, I would better be able to contribute by being in the Navy."

In Lower Manhattan this week Gunnery Sgt. Duane Silvera, who is in charge of Marine recruiting in Manhattan, welcomed Mr. Manin, the Kazakhstan native, into his office near City Hall to go over some final preparations before he starts basic training at Parris Island, S.C.

Mr. Manin said that his wife — an American citizen whom he married in 1999 — had mixed feelings. And his parents, who still live in his hometown of Petropavlovsk, were uncomfortable with his decision because they know of too many young men who never came back or were disabled after the Soviet war with Afghanistan.

But he was unbowed. He talked excitedly about becoming an infantryman, maybe doing reconnaissance work, maybe using his fluency in Kazakh (which is similar to Uzbek), Russian, Polish and Czech.

"I've been asking that I can go to Afghanistan to participate," Mr. Manin said.

His brother, Pacha, a 20-year-old who is now studying English at Fordham, wanted to enlist, too. But he is here on a student visa and does not have a green card — not yet. But Sergeant Silvera, 35, said that if Pacha Manin gets his green card, he would be a prime candidate. After all, Sergeant Silvera himself was a permanent resident and Jamaican citizen when he enlisted in the Marines.

Fast Track to Citizenship Is Cut Off for Some Military Recruits

BY MIRIAM JORDAN | SEPT. 15, 2017

MOHAMMED ANWAR enlisted in April 2016 in the United States military through a program that promised him a fast track to citizenship. His ship date for basic training, expected within six months, was postponed twice. "It was common knowledge that there were delays because of new security checks," said the 27-year-old Pakistani national, who lives in Jersey City.

Each month he donned a uniform and, as required, attended drill training with his Army Reserve unit in Connecticut.

Last week, Mr. Anwar got a call from his recruiter informing him that his enlistment had been terminated. "I was shocked, confused and angry that the United States government didn't keep up with its commitment to me," said Mr. Anwar, who was to work as a nurse.

The reason behind the decision to cut Mr. Anwar from the military remains unclear to him.

In the last week, recruiters have rescinded contracts for an unknown number of foreign nationals who had signed up for Military Accessions Vital to the National Interest, or Mavni, a program introduced in 2009 to attract immigrants with certain language and other skills that are in short supply into the armed forces.

More than 4,000 Mavni recruits have been in limbo since late last year, when the Department of Defense began introducing additional vetting. The protracted process has indefinitely delayed basic training for many enlistees, making it more difficult for recruiters to meet their targets. Recruiting stations are flooded with calls from many concerned that their lawful presence in the country could lapse while they await clearance.

Many Mavni recruits have been airing their concerns on Facebook. In interviews, some said they feared they could be deported.

An Army recruiter speaking to a potential recruit about paperwork requirements.

H.J. Zhu, a Chinese national who signed an enlistment contract in January 2016, said that he has been calling his recruiter constantly because his student visa expires in two months and he has yet to receive a date to report for basic training.

"Emotionally, I can't move forward with my life," said Mr. Zhu, 27, who has master's degrees in engineering from Columbia University and the University of Wyoming. "I am sure my contract is on the verge of being rescinded," he added, because enlistees must report to training within two years of signing a contract.

Paul Haverstick, a Pentagon spokesman, confirmed that the Army must discharge recruits who have not shipped to initial military training within two years.

"Unfortunately, some Mavni recruits have been unable to complete the increased security screening required by the Department of Defense to ship to training within two years of enlistment," he said, adding that the Army is still seeking ways to help those who have been affected.

"The Mavnis have become a huge problem for the recruiting command because they can't ship out to their training until they complete mandated background checks," said Margaret Stock, a retired lieutenant colonel in the Army Reserve who helped create the program. "If they can't ship out, they aren't doing the Army any good."

Ankit Gajurel, a Nepalese mechanical engineer who enlisted in the Army Reserve in May 2016, recently had his training date postponed for the second time. But several of his references had been contacted by security officials, and he had been told by his recruiter that his "counterintelligence interview," one of the last steps in the vetting process, would be scheduled for November.

"I was hopeful and happy things were moving," said Mr. Gajurel, 24, who lives in Minneapolis.

Instead, last week his recruiter phoned him to say that he was a "Mavni loss" and instructed him to turn in his military identification and stop attending training drills with his unit in Colorado. "I felt blindsided when that came over the phone," Mr. Gajurel said.

Ms. Stock said that with the end of the fiscal year approaching, the military offered "loss forgiveness" to recruiters of Mavni soldiers, a bureaucratic incentive to cancel their contracts so that they do not count against their performance.

Since 2009, more than 10,000 immigrants, mostly individuals on student or employment-based visas, have enlisted mainly in the Army. Mr. Anwar and Mr. Gajurel both came to the United States on student visas and then secured temporary work visas.

"I thought this would give me the opportunity to better myself and build my life in the United States as a citizen," Mr. Gajurel said.

Typically, participants in the program are sworn in as citizens after completing basic training, without having to first obtain a green card or permanent residency, making the program the quickest path to citizenship available. In exchange, they serve eight years in the military. They can lose their citizenship if they fail to serve honorably.

The program's success stories include Paul Chelimo, a native of Kenya who won a silver medal for the United States in the 2016 Olympics in Rio de Janeiro; Saral Shrestha, a Nepalese national, who was named the United States Army soldier of the year; and Dr. Marco Ladino, originally from Colombia, who works at the V.A. hospital in Miami.

Many have served as interpreters on military missions to Africa, Asia and the Middle East, or helped fill shortages of health professionals, like dentists. They also have trained American soldiers in language and culture.

Supporters of the program have advocated its expansion, saying it attracts a high caliber of recruits at a time when it is especially difficult to bring in well-educated, high-skilled Americans.

But critics have expressed concerns that terrorists could infiltrate it. There has never been a Mavni recruit charged with terrorism. However, dozens of native-born recruits have been charged with terrorism.

The program, which is renewed annually, has been suspended in the past.

Shortly after the November 2009 killing of 13 people at Fort Hood in Texas by an Army psychiatrist, an American-born son of immigrants, the program was suspended for about two years pending additional security reviews.

Immigrants with legal residency have long been eligible to join the military, but a law passed in the wake of the Sept. 11, 2001, attacks allows other documented immigrants to join if it is in the nation's vital interest. Mavni applicants must have lived legally in the country for at least two years to be eligible.

Immigrants currently represent about 13.5 percent of the United States population. They constituted 18 percent of the Army soldiers in World War I and 43 percent of the Union Army during the Civil War. Immigrants represented 5 percent of those in the armed forces and about 8 percent of Army recruits last year.

In Dad's Footsteps, and Flight Suit

BY CHRIS HEDGES | DEC. 19, 2002

WHEN JEREMY D. SCOTT was 10, his father, a United States Army helicopter pilot, was shot down by rebels in El Salvador and killed.

The boy played out his grief on the living room floor. He set up plastic soldiers that fired away at a pretend helicopter. Then he swooped down with his toy gunship to wipe out enemy troops. No helicopters crashed when he played. In his games the helicopter pilots always won. The soldiers, little green plastic men, always lay scattered about, only to be righted again for another battle.

"Maybe I played a little rougher than other kids," Mr. Scott said. "Maybe my emotions were held in, coming out in big lump sums. Things built up. I was explosive. It was tough to watch fathers play with their sons. I don't know when I really got over it. Maybe when I began daily devotions."

He lived through a decade of anger and mistrust. Now 22, Mr. Scott said he still finds it difficult to cope with the fact that there are things about the mission the government cannot tell his family, such as where his father was flying and why he was in combat.

"I did not accept that my dad could be taken away," he said. "At first I was angry at the Army. I blamed the Army for taking him from me."

But the pull of devotion and the sense of duty would prove greater than his anger. For Mr. Scott, the struggle to rekindle the spark of his father's life and career translated into following the same path. Four years ago, it took him to West Point. This spring, Cadet Scott plans to graduate, then go on to flight school.

"My mother is a little wary about me going into aviation after what happened to her husband," he said. "But she has not opposed it. She just tells me it is dangerous."

He conceded that it has not been an easy journey; indeed, the twinges of pain are evident as he nervously wrings his hands as he speaks about the loss. But he sees his route as one that allows him to validate not only his own life but also that of his father. And giving in to anger, turning on the military profession that led to his father's death, was a negation he was not prepared to endure. In the end, Cadet Scott found that one of the most straightforward of the commandments — one that many can fulfill without great sacrifice — profoundly shaped his destiny.

"I do believe that through my life I am honoring my father," Cadet Scott said. "For the most part I believe that any little boy growing up wishes to honor his father and make him proud. I remember my father telling myself and my mother that if I was to ever join the military to be an officer. Not only am I going to be an officer but I am graduating from a prestigious military academy. My father would be proud of my determination and ability to make it through West Point."

He carries in his wallet a high school picture of his father, Daniel S. Scott, a picture that his mother gave to him when his father died. In his desk he keeps copies of the military reports on the incident, filled with stilted jargon and cold descriptions of wounds and bodies. His father, according to a report dated Jan. 4, 1991, and issued by the Armed Forces Medical Examiners Office, "sustained blunt force injuries to the neck and chest resulting in incapacitation, unconsciousness and hypovolemic shock."

"CW4 Scott," the report reads, "died of injuries from the crash."

The two other American soldiers on board were executed by rebel gunmen after being pulled from the wreckage, the report stated.

"I don't speak about it much," Cadet Scott said. "A lot of the other cadets don't even know that my father passed away or the circumstances. I don't want to make them feel uncomfortable."

His father was a Christian who attended the Wyoming Bible Institute and Bob Jones University. "He had a big booming voice," his son said, "a preacher's voice."

By the time his father was stationed in Central America, flying helicopters in El Salvador for American military advisers to the Salvadoran army, his contact with his son was mostly through letters. His father diligently wrote him two or three times a week and did the same for his mother and four sisters. The stacks of letters are now small personal treasure-troves.

"He called me Buddy," Cadet Scott said. "He would tell me to take care of my mother and sisters, that I was the man of the house. I was only 8 or 9 years old.

"The postcards he sent me were pictures of helicopters," Cadet Scott said. "I reread them a year ago."

But the cards and letters had asides and offhand comments that disturbed the son. His father mentioned that he could hear shooting in the streets near the air base. And in the last letter he described how one of the helicopters had limped back "full of bullet holes."

"He asked me to pray for him to have strength," Cadet Scott said.

He remembers flashes of the funeral service, like star bursts. The bright sunlight in the cemetery in San Antonio, the 21-gun salute, the array of men in uniform, the casket with the flag and air medal for valor, the way everyone was hushed and quiet, and the effort by his grandfather and uncle, both preachers, to come to terms with the death.

"My grandfather said at the funeral that he was proud to be an American," Cadet Scott said, "and while it sounds like a cliché, that got to us. Those words hit my family pretty hard."

Even after what happened, Jeremy Scott liked war movies. He drew "dark pictures." His family, despite the loss, found structure and meaning in religious and military traditions.

These worlds offered an anchor, a sense of purpose, an unquestioned and noble call to duty, to God and country. For him, as for much of his family, these religious and patriotic demands were intimately intertwined.

"My grandfather and one of my uncles were marines," Cadet Scott said. "Even before my dad died I was sure I would enter the military. I always wanted to emulate my father."

When he was 16, able to put aside his anger at the Army, he went to the basement and tried on his father's old flight suit. His father was a large man, 6 feet 4 inches tall and 240 pounds. The flight suit hung on his son's thin frame like a bilious drape. The teenager put it back in the closet. In the spring, when Cadet Scott is scheduled to graduate from West Point and head to flight school, he will take it out again, he said.

He already has his father's flight glasses in his dormitory room. He is now 6-foot-3 and 206 pounds, or in his words "not quite there yet." But he is there enough to wear the suit. He is there enough to fly.

The peripatetic life of the Army, in which he and his family moved from base to base every few years, continued even after his father died. They seemed rootless, adrift, waiting in some sense to go home again.

"It was habit," he said. "We had to pick up and move. The Army gave all of us a sense of order, a lifestyle. Things were set down. You do not second-guess things in the military. It is a structured environment."

Cadet Scott defines himself as a Christian. He reads the Bible nearly every day and is part of the Bible study group at the academy. He trusts, he said, in the will of God and has learned to accept what happens in life as part of a divine plan. He said he is positive that his father is in heaven.

"I try to have good morals," he said. "I refrain from bad language. I do not believe in sex before marriage. I don't like this drive to push church out of society, to do things like take prayer out of schools."

In 1993, the rebel soldiers who shot down the helicopter and executed the two other crew members went on trial in El Salvador. No one from his family, despite invitations, felt like attending the trial. The men, sentenced and convicted, were later released as part of a general amnesty.

War, as it did for his father, looms over him. He said he knows that he, too, may have to fly into combat. He, too, may take hostile fire. But Cadet Scott said he was prepared to fulfill his duty to God and country, and live out what he considers his destiny.

"God took my father away for a reason," he said. "I might not have matured the way I did. I might not be here.

"It was God's plan."

15 Years Ago, I Helped Start a War That Hasn't Ended

BY MATT UFFORD | MARCH 20, 2018

WHEN I DEPLOYED to Iraq in 2003, there was no war. We had to start it.

As a lieutenant in charge of six tanks (four active-duty crews, two reserve), I gave a preinvasion talk to my platoon before rolling out. It was 15 years ago, and I was 24 — older than all but two of the 23 crewmen. It was a moment I had long fantasized about, inspired by the fist-pumping motivational speeches that rouse the troops in war movies like "Gladiator" and "Patton."

Behind a line of tanks, on a stretch of Kuwaiti sand as flat and featureless as my courage, I adopted a folksy tone. "I know y'all were probably looking forward to a big 'Braveheart' talk, but you know me — I'm not one to speechify." I paused, tried to stop my voice from shaking and failed. "I'm just like the rest of you: I've never been to combat, so I don't know what it's like. But I want to tell you all that it's O.K. to be scared." I'm not sure whom I was trying to convince more: my Marines or myself. "What's not O.K. is to let that fear overcome you. No panicking. We're all well trained, and as long as we go with our training and make quick decisions, we're gonna accomplish the mission and be fine. Tank commanders, you know what I expect." That was it. No one responded with a battle cry.

Of the 80 or so Marines in Delta Company, First Tank Battalion, only one of us had ever seen combat: a gunnery sergeant who fought in Desert Storm. His face was creased and leathery from a decade in the Mojave outpost of Twentynine Palms, and he had the unhurried gait of a man whose cartilage was shot from a career of clambering on and off no-skid steel. Soon many of us would look more like him than our selves.

We spent the weeks before the invasion in Kuwait waiting for orders, fighting off boredom. We adjusted the sights of our tanks, banged on the tracks with heavy tools, went over the assault plan, pored through satellite imagery, cleaned our weapons, practiced speed drills with gas masks and still had more empty hours than busy ones. We joked that we wanted the war to start just for a break from the monotony.

We filled the time with card games, pranks, rumors and — occasionally, quietly — our thoughts and fears about combat. My friend Travis Carlson had a specific fear of being shot through the neck. I couldn't decide if I was more afraid of death or of the general unknown of what waited for us once we crossed the border. Nothing loomed larger, though, than the desire to live up to the storied history of the Marine Corps. I didn't need to stand shoulder to shoulder with the legend of Chesty Puller and his five Navy Crosses or the corps' long list of Medal of Honor recipients, but I couldn't let them down either.

The case for the invasion was thin — or rather, it was thick, but, we now know, filled with faulty intelligence, half-truths and a fervor for war that was unsated by the conflict in Afghanistan. Back in the United States, President George W. Bush told the nation on March 19 that it was time to free the people of Iraq and "defend the world from grave danger." Within hours, thousands of troops, including my battalion, crossed the border to look for Saddam Hussein's weapons of mass destruction.

Our company commander stressed that we should exact only as much harm as the mission required, but a tank is not a scalpel. When we drove across a field, newly planted crops flew skyward behind our vehicles in great roostertails of earth. When we provided supporting fire to an engineer detonating mines, we felled trees with our machine guns. Inside the tank, we hardly felt a bump when we crushed cars under our treads. We brought war everywhere we went.

The pace was relentless: a race to an objective, a brief engagement — tanks have a way of ending battles quickly — and then back on the highway. We drove all day and all night, from Basra to Nasiriyah to Diwaniyah, stopping only to refuel. Over the course of a week, I slept 10 hours. No one up the chain of command seemed to care about sleep until one of Charlie Company's tanks drove off a bridge over the Euphrates in the middle of the night. It settled in the riverbed upside-down, and the four Marines inside died.

We doglegged east to Numaniyah, then continued to push northwest on Highway 6. That's where my friend Brian McPhillips of Second Tank Battalion was fatally shot in the head, but I wouldn't hear the news for another two weeks. Information rarely travels laterally in war. I was a few miles from the ambush that killed him when I learned that my platoon would lead the battalion over the Diyala River and into Baghdad.

The bridge was partly destroyed. Two-thirds of the way to the far side, a chunk of the span was gone, leaving pieces of exposed rebar and a clear view to the water below. Combat engineers laid a makeshift bridge over the gap. I asked the engineer lieutenant if it would hold a tank's weight. "I think so," he said.

As the platoon commander, I could dictate which tank went over first, but it wasn't really a choice. It had barely been a week since Charlie Company's Marines drowned in the Euphrates; I left the hatch of my cupola all the way open, prepared to jump free of the vehicle if it went in the water.

As we came over the crest of the bridge, a man on the far side of the river fired an AK-47 at us. This was inconvenient. I was trying to guide our driver onto the engineer's bridge while scanning the landscape for other threats; being shot at felt gratuitous.

"Co-ax, fire," I said.

"On the way," my gunner replied, and ended someone's life with the tank's 7.62-millimeter coaxial machine gun.

As he fired, I caught sight of a Soviet-made T-72 tank dug into a defensive position. I grabbed the override to rotate the turret while giving a hasty fire command to my gunner. The thunderous boom echoed across the battlefield, and I saw the orange spark of steel on steel. Secondary explosions followed as the T-72's ammunition cooked off. On the radio, I reported the kills and called off the artillery mission, which was well inside the "danger close" range of 600 meters. I could feel the overpressure from the bursting shells, a concussive force that shook my cheeks.

"Hey, sir?" It was my driver. "Are those mines?"

We had driven across the bridge into a minefield. It ended up being a long day.

Baghdad fell on April 9. After the resistance on the outskirts of the city, we expected a devastating battle on urban terrain. Instead, we rolled into the capital and were greeted by cheers. It felt as if my chest might burst from relief and pride: The job was done, and all my men were alive. I had been a part of the longest inland assault in Marine Corps history.

Ten days later, First Tank Battalion left the capital; our vehicles were "too aggressive" of a posture for the peacekeeping mission to come. The occupation needed military police officers and translators; we had 70-ton vehicles with high-explosive anti-tank rounds. It

TYLER HICKS/THE NEW YORK TIMES

U.S. troops keeping watch as the Ministry of Transportation burned in Baghdad, Iraq, on April 9, 2003.

seemed like a rash decision — and indeed, tanks would be a mainstay of the Marine mission in Iraq for years to come — but that didn't stop us from whooping with excitement as we left the city. The occupation was someone else's problem now.

Fifteen years later, the invasion is a footnote to the war, and the aftermath is filled with too much death and dishonor for me to ever regret leaving the service without another deployment. But there was a moment — before Abu Ghraib, before Falluja, before the Haditha massacre, or the Surge, or the drawdown, or ISIS — that I still cherish. On the day we rolled into Baghdad as victors, First Tank Battalion encamped in the shadow of the giant turquoise dome of the Al-Shaheed Monument, enjoying the protection of the man-made lakes around it. We were abuzz with the joy of being alive and having accomplished our mission. I shared a kettle of coffee with one of my sergeants, and I told him I wanted to come back to Baghdad one day to see what it might look like in peace and prosperity. As the sun set on a liberated city, golden light turned the dusty sidewalks to warm coral, and for a moment it felt as if the war were over.

MATT UFFORD is a freelance writer and video host who served in the Marine Corps from 2000 to 2004.

An Injustice in the Bergdahl Sentence

OPINION | BY ROB CUTHBERT | NOV. 3, 2017

IN THE VIEW of many people, Sgt. Bowe Bergdahl got off easy. His sentence for desertion and misbehavior before the enemy in Afghanistan in 2009, which was handed down Friday, included a dishonorable discharge and no jail time.

Sergeant Bergdahl faced the possibility of life in a military prison, so his chief defense lawyer expressed "tremendous relief" at the sentence. But a dishonorable discharge is also a type of life sentence, a perpetual exile from the resources and communities that veterans, especially prisoners of war, need to heal and to reconcile with society.

Eight years ago, Sergeant Bergdahl intentionally walked away from his post in Afghanistan. He had a highly unusual reason for leaving: He was marching to another base to blow the whistle on commanders that he believed were incompetent and dangerous. After less than a day of travel, he was captured by the Taliban.

After almost five years in Taliban captivity, I was doubtful that the Army would give Sergeant Bergdahl a life sentence; even the prosecutors capped their request at 14 years. He was guilty of crimes that led to the grave injury of other service members, but after years of working with veterans with less-than-honorable discharges, I thought about how Sergeant Bergdahl, a disabled prisoner of war, would lead the rest of his civilian life. If he was given a dishonorable discharge at 31 years old, how could he mend his wounds, attempt to pay his moral and civic debts, and contribute to the nation?

At a preliminary hearing, Terrence Russell, a senior Department of Defense expert in personnel recovery, testified that Sergeant Bergdahl was held "in conditions that if it were a dog, you'd be thrown in jail for pet abuse." He was tortured and beaten. For three years, he lived in a seven-foot cube. For three and a half years, he had uncontrollable diarrhea that he scrubbed off his body with dirt and washed off with urine. According to Mr. Russell, the conditions of Sergeant Bergdahl's sadistic captivity rated among the "most horrible" the military had seen in 60 years; as a prisoner, Mr. Russell said, Sergeant Bergdahl "had to fight off the enemy alone for four years and 11 months."

Sergeant Bergdahl is home now, but in many ways he's never left the pillory. He returned to rampant slander and unsubstantiated rumors of treason. President Obama had swapped prisoners for Bergdahl's release, but would not spend the political capital to resolve his case. And, in an egregious act of unlawful command influence, President Donald J. Trump maintained that Bergdahl was a "dirty rotten traitor" who should be shot.

As a matter of propriety, military commanders — including the commander in chief — are supposed to refrain from influencing pending matters of military justice, since their subordinates are expected to act without bias. Col. Jeffrey R. Nance, the sentencing judge, acknowledged the import of Trump's toxic statements, but despite the protests of Sergeant Bergdahl's lawyers, Colonel Nance felt that he could remain unbiased and refused to dismiss Sergeant Bergdahl's case.

Sergeant Bergdahl and future troops would have benefited from a swift condemnation of Mr. Trump's de facto attempts at judge-tampering. Sergeant Bergdahl's sentence is under final review by military authorities, including the Army Court of Criminal Appeals, and on Friday, the president continued to try to exert influence, calling the sentence, as it stands, a "total disgrace to our country and our military."

Sergeant Bergdahl will soon receive his dishonorable discharge. He will be a civilian with significant physical disabilities, post-traumatic stress disorder and a very high risk of suicide. Of the six types of discharge, dishonorable is the most punishing. When he is discharged, Sergeant Bergdahl will be denied almost all reintegration benefits — including comprehensive medical — and he will also not be recognized as a veteran by the federal government. He will come back wounded to family and friends who love him, without the expert medical care of a country that must balance its responsibility to punish him and to heal him.

The trajectory of Sergeant Bergdahl's career speaks to tragic and avoidable flaws in the military mental health care system. Sergeant Bergdahl suffers from schizotypal personality disorder, and it was only after a mental health-related discharge from the Coast Guard that the Army enlisted him on a medical waiver. If his illness had been treated before his crimes, he could have been eligible for an honorable discharge with benefits. The available military record shows that when Sergeant Bergdahl left his place of duty, he was an exemplary, idealistic young soldier who lived with mental illness, not a traitor.

Sergeant Bergdahl's offenses put the lives of fellow soldiers at risk. At his court-martial, prosecutors highlighted several profound and permanent injuries to troops during the search for Sergeant Bergdahl, but Army investigators have stated that none were killed during attempts to find him.

Sergeant Bergdahl has expressed profound remorse and admitted that he "made a horrible mistake" when he left his post. In his skewed logic, he believed that he "was trying to help," and it was never his intention "for anyone to be hurt."

There is still a chance for the military to review and reduce the sentence, but if they choose to uphold it, Sergeant Bergdahl deserves the immediate intervention of civilian-led authorities who have the power to use clemency to grant a less severe discharge. By definition, clemency is an act of mercy. It would not absolve Sergeant Bergdahl of guilt, but both the secretary of the Army and the Army Board for Correction of Military Records have the authority to use it to give him a less severe discharge that preserves the benefits that he needs to heal and to lead a long life.

Clemency is rare, but if Sergeant Bergdahl's voluminous public record is a guide, I believe that he could present a strong case. Authorities must consider mitigating factors, including his in-service conduct, wounds he received in action, his mental health, and whether he met normal military accession standards.

Sergeant Bergdahl's military service cannot be reduced to his crimes. I would argue that his profound and unexpected contribution to the military truly began the day he was captured.

Although Sergeant Bergdahl had left his post and put others in danger, he fought, resisted, collected a "gold mine" of intelligence on the enemy and — at great risk to his life — tried to escape multiple times, including a daring attempt in which he eluded the Taliban for eight and a half days. In time, his exemplary service to our country as a prisoner of war will direct and inspire the survival of other P.O.W.s.

If necessary, members of Congress should send a bipartisan letter to the secretary of the Army in support of a less severe discharge for Sergeant Bergdahl that ensures medical benefits. Moreover, this year, Congress must pass a bill that ensures medical care and disability benefits for all former prisoners of war, regardless of discharge status.

Sergeant Bergdahl's permanently injured, would-be rescuers are selfless and brave. But we must remember that — regardless of Sergeant Bergdahl's tragic and unnecessary circumstances of capture — it was the enemies of America who tortured him and tried to kill those who sought to rescue him.

Sergeant Bergdahl's misguided crimes can't be forgotten, but his punishment must have limits. In light of his courage in captivity, we must be able to balance two compatible martial values: honor and mercy.

ROB CUTHBERT is an Army veteran who formerly managed the military discharge upgrade clinic at the Veteran Advocacy Project of the Urban Justice Center.

Air Force Failed to Report Dozens
of Service Members to Gun Database

BY RICHARD A. OPPEL JR. | NOV. 28, 2017

DOZENS OF AIR FORCE service members charged with or convicted of serious crimes were never reported to the federal gun background-check database as required, Air Force officials said on Tuesday.

The revelation came after the Air Force disclosed that it had failed to report the domestic violence conviction of Devin P. Kelley, the gunman who opened fire at a church in Texas this month. Under federal law, Mr. Kelley's court-martial conviction for domestic assault should have prevented him from purchasing at a gun store the rifle he used in the attack, as well as other guns he acquired over the past four years.

After the Air Force admitted on Nov. 6 that officials at Holloman Air Force Base in New Mexico had failed to report the results of Mr. Kelley's court-martial to the federal background database, it began an investigation into how many other serious incidents had not been reported.

Although officials have only examined a portion of the cases, several dozen have already surfaced that were not reported but should have been.

"The error in the Kelley case was not an isolated incident and similar reporting lapses occurred at other locations," the Air Force said in a statement. "Although policies and procedures requiring reporting were in place, training and compliance measures were lacking."

Air Force officials say they are reviewing the results of the inquiry to date to assess whether to take any punitive action against personnel who failed to report Mr. Kelley's conviction.

The Air Force review is only one part of a wide-ranging investigation into the background-check reporting process underway inside the military and the Justice Department in the aftermath of the church massacre. Mr. Kelley, who pleaded guilty at a 2012 court-martial to assaulting his wife at the time and fracturing his stepson's skull, killed 25 people in Sutherland Springs, Tex., on Nov. 5. The victims included a pregnant women whose fetus also died.

Attorney General Jeff Sessions, citing the lapses in the Kelley case, last week ordered a federal review of the background-check database by the F.B.I. and the Bureau of Alcohol, Tobacco, Firearms and Explosives to ensure that the military and other federal agencies are reporting all required cases.

"The National Instant Criminal Background Check System is critical for us to be able to keep guns out of the hands of those that are prohibited from owning them," Mr. Sessions said. "The recent shooting in Sutherland Springs, Texas, revealed that relevant information may not be getting reported to the N.I.C.S. — this is alarming and it is unacceptable."

In addition to the Air Force investigation, the Pentagon's inspector general is looking into the handling of Mr. Kelley's court-martial conviction records and whether procedures are in place to ensure cases from other service branches are also sent to the database as required. The Army chief of staff, Gen. Mark Milley, said that he believed there were also a significant number of omissions of soldiers' records that should have been sent to the federal database.

And the number of cases that were not properly reported by the Air Force could grow: There have been about 60,000 incidents in the Air Force since 2002 involving service members that potentially should have been reported to the federal background-check database. All of those incidents are now being reviewed by Air Force officials to see which ones were required to be reported, and how many of those actually were. Air Force officials were unable to say on Tuesday how many of those 60,000 cases have gone through the review process so far.

While that review is expected to continue for several months, Air Force officials say they are moving to fix problems that prevented Mr. Kelley's conviction from being reported. And officials emphasized that they would continue to send previously unreported cases to the federal database as soon as they discover them.

Among other things, the new directive includes a requirement that personnel at the Air Force Office of Special Investigations must confirm that reportable cases have been entered into the federal database by seeing either a printout or a screenshot from the database.

Don Christensen, who was the chief prosecutor in the Air Force and is now president of Protect Our Defenders, a nonprofit group that supports greater protections for victims of sexual assault and domestic violence in the military, said the measures were long overdue.

"I'm not surprised that they are finding these lapses, because this was clearly never a priority in the past," Mr. Christensen said. "Earlier inspector general investigations found that they were not doing this properly, and the leadership never made it a priority to correct it."

Even if Mr. Kelley's conviction had been in the federal database, he could still have purchased a gun online or in person from private sellers not required to run a background check — an exemption known as the "gun show loophole."

In Texas, Claryce Holcombe, who lost eight family members in the attack, has filed a wrongful death claim against the Air Force over the death of her son, Bryan Holcombe, who was shot in the back and died on the floor of the church.

Ms. Holcombe's claim states that her son's death "was caused, in whole or in part, by the institutional failures" of the Pentagon and the Air Force, which negligently and recklessly "failed to report pertinent criminal arrest, conviction and military discharge information."

An Air Force spokeswoman said the Air Force does not comment on specific claims, but that every such claim is "thoroughly investigated and researched in accordance with established law and regulations."

Training Quick and Staffing Unfinished, Army Units Brace for Surging Taliban

BY THOMAS GIBBONS-NEFF | JAN. 26, 2018

WASHINGTON — They are being heralded as a key part of President Trump's new strategy to resolve the nearly 17-year war in Afghanistan. But their training has been cut short by months, and units are still short-staffed, as some of the estimated 1,000 additional military advisers prepare to arrive in Afghanistan in time for the spring fighting season, officials said.

The Army soldiers are deploying as the Pentagon begins shifting resources from the fight against the Islamic State in Iraq and Syria back to Afghanistan. As part of its new assault against an increasingly tenacious Taliban, the Trump administration is planning to send some of the advisers back to small bases scattered across rural parts of the country to help train Afghan forces.

The new brigade of advisers was formed in August and is based at Fort Benning, Ga. Two military officials said its leaders were still trying to ensure that each small team had enough soldiers to train Afghans.

One of those officials, and an additional one, said that the advisers' brigade was supposed to have around a year of training before deploying. Advisers in the new brigade are expected to begin deploying by early spring — roughly eight months after the brigade was created.

Additionally, a six-week Army course specifically for combat advisers was slashed to two weeks to more quickly cycle the American soldiers through training.

Earlier this month, the brigade's commander, Col. Scott Jackson, offered a blunt assessment about the difficulties to United States Central Command's top general, Joseph L. Votel, according to the military officials, who were familiar with the conversation and spoke on the condition of anonymity because they were not authorized to discuss it publicly. Central Command oversees combat operations in the Middle East.

Following that conversation, and another with some of the advisers, General Votel spoke with Gen. Mark A. Milley, the Army chief of staff, about the coming deployment in a private phone call.

General Milley has long made the units of advisers, known as Security Forces Assistance Brigades, one of his leading priorities. But the push to send the teams to the front, even with potential staffing shortages, comes as the American military deals with a series of crises, including two collisions of Navy ships in the Pacific last summer and several aviation crashes in the Marine Corps over the last year, that exposed readiness problems in the services.

Maj. Matthew E. Fontaine, a spokesman for the brigade, said, "We have enough soldiers to deploy." He said additional advisers, from Fort Drum, N.Y., were still being assigned to the unit. And he said many of the advisers had enough experience in war zones to adjust, despite the accelerated training schedule.

It was not unusual a decade ago, at the height of America's two wars in Iraq and Afghanistan, for infantry units to find themselves rushed to deploy with compacted training. Since 2009, small teams of United States troops have deployed across Afghanistan to teach the American way of war to local soldiers and police officers.

But the Army advisers who are part of Mr. Trump's strategy are being sent to outposts that will put them closer to the Taliban than most American soldiers have gone since 2014, with the exception of Special Operations troops, who receive rigorous training and are usually sent to the small bases for limited visits.

The advisers will help train Afghan forces, including marshaling air support and artillery when they are targeted by the Taliban, said one of the military officials who was familiar with the coming deployment.

Jason Dempsey, an adjunct senior fellow at the Center for a New American Security, warned that the Army advisers were being set up to fail — much the way ad hoc and untrained teams fell apart in earlier missions around Afghanistan.

"Even though they've been stood up and somewhat formalized, it's still a generic answer to a problem that requires a deep understanding of Afghan culture and politics," said Mr. Dempsey, who deployed twice to Afghanistan as an infantry officer, including as a combat adviser from 2012 to 2013.

He said the unit ran the risk of being judged by the American military's typical measure of progress: regaining territory from enemy groups through airstrikes.

"We're buying them time, but not addressing the underlying political dysfunction that makes them ineffective," Dempsey said of Afghan forces. "The Afghans continue to be beat by a force that doesn't need air power, so I'll believe the Afghan Army is competent when they don't need American air power."

The Afghan Air Force has grown in recent years, but still heavily relies on American troops and civilian advisers for training and maintenance. The Pentagon is sending more aircraft to battle zones to bolster the Afghans, coinciding with the uptick in airstrikes under Mr. Trump's new strategy.

Over the last four months, American warplanes dropped 1,874 munitions in Afghanistan, compared to 524 for the same period in 2016.

Faced with the increased airstrikes, militants last year launched more ambushes, insider attacks and assassinations instead of trying to hold territory, according to the third military official, who described parts of a National Ground Intelligence Center report that has not been publicly released.

Armed Afghan groups focused more on small arms attacks against American forces, wounding more than 150 troops in both explosive attacks and gunfire. Eleven were killed in combat in 2017.

The militants have also increased rocket and mortar attacks since 2016, prompting American forces to start to equip bases in southern Afghanistan with weapons to counter the indirect fire.

The Taliban have improved their ability to strike in the dark, often with captured American night vision devices or over-the-counter goggles, according to the officer's description of the government report. Taliban militants have more than doubled night raids since 2014, killing hundreds of Afghan troops.

And though the small teams of advisers are supposed to be capable of defending themselves, infantry soldiers are being sent to provide a ring of protection to their missions. Some of the force protection soldiers will deploy next month from Fort Carson, Colo.

An Army officer familiar with that deployment said the infantry soldiers were still collecting information about where they were headed. They are expected to land in Afghan towns and farmlands — places where American forces have not been stationed in years, and where they will probably clear roads of explosives and fight the Taliban.

The Warrior at the Mall

OPINION | BY PHIL KLAY | APRIL 14, 2018

"WE'RE AT WAR while America is at the mall."

I'm not sure when I first heard this in Iraq, but even back in 2007 it was already a well-worn phrase, the logical counterpart to George W. Bush's arguing after the Sept. 11 attacks that we must not let the terrorists frighten us to the point "where people don't shop."

Marines had probably started saying it as early as 2002. "We're at war while America is at the mall," some lance corporal muttered to another as they shivered against the winds rushing down the valleys in the Hindu Kush. "We're at war while America is at the mall," some prematurely embittered lieutenant told his platoon sergeant as they drove up to Nasiriyah in a light armored vehicle.

Whatever the case, when I heard it, it sounded right. Just enough truth mixed with self-aggrandizement to appeal to a man in his early 20s. Back home was shopping malls and strip clubs. Over here was death and violence and hope and despair. Back home was fast food and high-fructose corn syrup. Over here, we had bodies flooding the rivers of Iraq until people claimed it changed the taste of the fish. Back home they had aisles filled wall to wall with toothpaste, shaving cream, deodorant and body spray. Over here, sweating under the desert sun, we smelled terrible. We were at war, they were at the mall.

The old phrase popped back into my head recently while I was shopping for baby onesies on Long Island — specifically, in the discount section on the second floor of the Buy Buy Baby. Yes, I was at the mall, and America was still at war.

There's something bizarre about being a veteran of a war that doesn't end, in a country that doesn't pay attention. At this point, I've been out of the military far longer than I was in, and the weight I place on the value of military life versus civilian life has shifted radically. On the one hand, I haven't lost my certainty that Americans should be

paying more attention to our wars and that our lack of attention truly does cost lives.

"We've claimed war-weariness, or 'America First,' and turned a blind eye to the slaughter of 500,000 people and suffering of millions more," the former Marine Mackenzie Wolf pointed out in a March essay on America's unconscionable lack of action in Syria up to that point. On the other hand, I'm increasingly convinced that my youthful contempt for the civilians back home was not just misplaced, but obscene and, frankly, part of the problem.

After four United States soldiers assigned to the Army's Third Special Forces Group were killed in an ambush in Niger, the American public had a lot of questions. Why were they in combat in Niger? What was their mission? How do you pronounce "Niger"? Answering these questions would have required a complex, sustained discussion about how America projects force around the world, about expanding the use of Special Operations forces to 149 countries, and about whether we are providing those troops with well-thought-out missions and the resources to achieve them in the service of a sound and worthwhile national security strategy.

And since our troops were in Niger in a continuation of an Obama administration policy that began in 2013, it also would have meant discussing the way that administration ramped up "supervise, train and assist" missions in Africa, how it often tried to blur the line between advisory and combat missions to avoid public scrutiny, and how the Trump administration appears to have followed in those footsteps. It would have required, at a bare minimum, not using the deaths as material for neat, partisan parables.

Naturally, we didn't have that conversation. Instead, a Democratic congresswoman who heard the president's phone call to the widow of one of the fallen soldiers informed the news media that Mr. Trump had ineptly told the grieving woman that her husband "knew what he signed up for."

Quickly, Americans shifted from a discussion of policy to a symbolic battle over which side, Democratic or Republican, wasn't respecting soldiers enough. Had the president disrespected the troops with his comment? Had Democrats disrespected the troops by trying to use a condolence call for political leverage? Someone clearly had run afoul of an odd form of political correctness, "patriotic correctness."

Since, as recent history has shown us, violating the rules of patriotic correctness is a far worse sin in the eyes of the American public than sending soldiers to die uselessly, the political battle became intense, and the White House was forced to respond. And since in a symbolic debate of this kind nothing is better than an old soldier, the retired Marine general and current chief of staff, John Kelly, was trotted out in an Oct. 19 news conference to defend the president.

He began powerfully enough, describing what happens to the bodies of soldiers killed overseas, and bringing up his own still painful memories of the loss of his son, who died in Afghanistan in 2010. He spoke with pride of the men and women in uniform.

But then, in an all too common move, he transitioned to expressing contempt for the civilian world. He complained that nothing seemed to be sacred in America anymore, not women, not religion, not even "the dignity of life." He told the audience that service members volunteer even though "there's nothing in our country anymore that seems to suggest that selfless service to the nation is not only appropriate, but required." He said veterans feel "a little bit sorry" for civilians who don't know the joys of service.

To cap things off, he took questions only from reporters who knew families who had lost loved ones overseas. The rest of the journalists, and by extension the rest of the American public who don't know any Gold Star families, were effectively told they had no place in the debate.

Such disdain for those who haven't served and yet dare to have opinions about military matters is nothing new for Mr. Kelly. In a 2010 speech after the death of his son, Mr. Kelly improbably claimed that we were winning in Afghanistan, but that "you wouldn't know it because successes go unreported" by members of the " 'know it all' chattering class" who "always seem to know better, but have never themselves been in the arena." And he argued that to oppose the war, which our current secretary of defense last year testified to Congress we were not winning, meant "slighting our warriors and mocking their commitment to the nation."

This is a common attitude among a significant faction of veterans. As one former member of the Special Forces put it in a social media post responding to the liberal outcry over the deaths in Niger, "We did what we did so that you can be free to naïvely judge us, complain about the manner in which we kept you safe" and "just all around live your worthless sponge lives." His commentary, which was liked and shared thousands of times, is just a more embittered form of the sentiment I indulged in as a young lieutenant in Iraq.

It can be comforting to reverse the feelings of hopelessness and futility that come with fighting seemingly interminable, strategically dubious wars by enforcing a hierarchy of citizenship that puts the veteran and those close to him on top, and everyone else far, far below.

But John Kelly's contempt for modern civilian life wasn't a pep talk voiced in a Humvee traveling down an Iraqi highway, or at a veterans' reunion in a local bar. He was speaking to the American people, with the authority of a retired general, on behalf of the president of the United States of America. And he was letting us know our place.

Those with questions about military policy are being put in their place more and more often these days. When reporters later asked the White House press secretary, Sarah Huckabee Sanders, about some of Mr. Kelly's claims, which had proved false, she said, "If you want to get into a debate with a four-star Marine general, I think that's highly inappropriate." It was an echo of the way Sean Spicer tried to short-circuit debate about the death of a Navy SEAL in Yemen by claiming that anyone who questioned the success of the raid "owes an apology" to the fallen SEAL.

Serious discussion of foreign policy and the military's role within it is often prohibited by this patriotic correctness. Yet, if I have authority to speak about our military policy it's because I'm a citizen responsible for participating in self-governance, not because I belonged to a warrior caste.

If what I say deserves to be taken seriously, it's because I've taken the time out of my worthless sponge life as a concerned American civilian to form a worthy opinion. Which means that although it is my patriotic duty to afford men like John Kelly respect for his service, and for the grief he has endured as the father of a son who died for our country, that is not where my responsibility as a citizen ends.

I must also assume that our military policy is of direct concern to me, personally. And if a military man tries to leverage the authority and respect he is afforded to voice contempt for a vast majority of Americans, if he tries to stifle their exercise of self-governance by telling them that to question the military strategy of our generals and our political leaders is a slight to our troops, it's my patriotic duty to tell him to go pound sand.

If we don't do this, we risk our country slipping further into the practice of a fraudulent form of American patriotism, where "soldiers" are sacred, the work of actual soldiering is ignored and the pageantry of military worship sucks energy away from the obligations of citizenship.

I understand why politicians and writers and institutions choose to employ the trope of veterans when it comes to arguing for their causes. Support for our military remains high at a time when respect for almost every other institution is perilously low, so pushing a military angle as a wedge makes a certain kind of sense. But our peacetime institutions are not justified by how they intermittently intersect with national security concerns — it's the other way around. Our military is justified only by the civic life and values it exists to defend. This is why George Washington, in his Farewell Orders to the Continental Army, told his troops to "carry with them into civil society the most conciliating dispositions" and "prove themselves not less virtuous and useful as citizens than they have been persevering and victorious as soldiers."

Besides, let's not pretend that living a civilian life — and living it well — isn't hard. A friend of mine, an officer in the Army Reserves, told me that one of his greatest leadership challenges came not overseas, but when a deployment to Afghanistan got canceled and his men were called to the difficult and often tedious work of being husbands, fathers, members of a community.

My wife and I are raising two sons — the older one is 2 years old, the little one 6 months. And as we follow our national politics with occasional disgust, amusement, horror and hope, we regularly talk about the sort of qualities we want to impress upon our boys so they can be good citizens, and how we can help cultivate in them a sense of service, of gratitude for the blessings they have, and a desire to give back. It's a daunting responsibility. Right now, though, the day-to-day work of raising these kids doesn't involve a lot of lofty rhetoric about service. It involves drool, diapers and doing the laundry. For me, it means being that most remarkable, and somehow most unremarkable of things — a dad.

Which is how I found myself that day, less a Marine veteran than a father, shopping with the other parents at Buy Buy Baby, recalling that old saying, "We're at war while America is at the mall." I wondered about the anonymous grunt poet who coined it. Whoever he was, there's a good chance that even by the time I heard it, he'd already done his four years and gotten out.

Maybe he'd left the Corps, settled into civilian life. Maybe he was in school. Perhaps he was working as a schoolteacher, or as a much-derided civil servant in some corner of our government. Perhaps he found that work more satisfying, more hopeful and of more obvious benefit to his country than the work he'd done in our mismanaged wars.

Or perhaps, if he was as lucky as I have been, he was in some other mall doing exactly what I was — trying to figure out the difference between 6M and 3-6M baby onesies. If so, I wish him well.

PHIL KLAY (@PhilKlay) is the author of the short story collection "Redeployment" and a veteran of the United States Marine Corps.

Sergeant Sues Defense Dept. Over 'Outdated' H.I.V. Policies

BY DAVE PHILIPPS | MAY 31, 2018

ARMY SGT. NICK HARRISON learned he was infected with H.I.V. six years ago, but the once fatal diagnosis has barely changed his routine at work or at home because he keeps the virus in check with a once-a-day pill. The only thing H.I.V. crippled was his military career. The military bars anyone with the virus that causes AIDS from joining. Policies crafted in the 1980s allow troops who contract the disease while in the military to stay as long as they remain otherwise healthy, but bars them from deploying in nearly all cases.

The question of how to treat healthy troops who have H.I.V. was hardly an issue a few decades ago, when few with the infection lived long. Now that they can lead long and healthy lives, however, the restrictions meant to control a deadly epidemic have stifled careers. Many have been shut out from coveted specialties or denied promotions. And under a new policy that requires troops to be readily deployable or be discharged, nearly 1,823 otherwise healthy troops with H.I.V. may be forced to leave the military.

Now Sergeant Harrison, who served 18 years in the Army and National Guard and deployed to Afghanistan and Kuwait, is suing the Defense Department, arguing that the H.I.V. policies are outdated and discriminatory and have cost him a promotion to captain.

"In the Army we are taught that we are all one team, and as long as you can fulfill the mission, any differences don't matter," Sergeant Harrison said in an interview. "These policies seem to fundamentally oppose that core philosophy."

In a complaint filed in United States District Court for the Eastern District of Virginia this week, lawyers from the public interest groups Lambda Legal and Outserve-SLDN, who represent the sergeant, say that the blanket policies discriminate against people with H.I.V. and violate the constitutional right to equal protection.

Military rules, the complaint argues, have not kept pace with tremendous progress in H.I.V. treatment, including a widely available oral medication that can keep virus levels so low that people can live with no symptoms and almost no risk of passing on the disease to others.

"It's outdated policy based on unfounded fears that doesn't recognize all the advances we've made," said Scott A. Schoettes, one of the lawyers representing the sergeant.

The Defense Department declined to comment on the lawsuit, but in a statement said its policies on H.I.V. are "evidence-based, medically accurate, and are reviewed regularly and updated as practices, guidelines, and standards of care evolve."

The military has long disqualified recruits for a broad range of medical conditions that could impact performance, including bad knees, heel spurs, diabetes and even peanut allergies. But it also regularly grants waivers for people who can show their condition will not affect their duties or pose a hazard to other troops. H.I.V. was added to the list of disqualifying conditions in 1985 as the military scrambled to control the spread of the disease during the peak of the AIDS crisis. That year, the military began regularly testing all troops. Those who tested positive were sidelined. Pilots were grounded. Leaders were pulled out of command positions. On one Army post in Texas, H.I.V.-positive troops were quarantined in barracks that soldiers quickly began calling "the leper colony."

"Anyone who tested positive stayed in the military, and we treated them. It was seen as the compassionate thing to do," said Dr. Craig Hendrix, an infectious disease specialist at Johns Hopkins University who ran the Air Force's H.I.V. monitoring program for most of the 1990s. "But the expectation was that they would soon become too sick to perform their duties and be medically discharged. No one was expected to last long. At the time the best drugs would only buy a year or two."

Dr. Hendrix, who has been out of the military for nearly 20 years, was surprised to hear that policy has changed little.

"It's one of many, many conditions fully compatible with being on active duty," he said. "I suspect there are a number of people in the military taking a pill each day for blood pressure or cholesterol. This is hardly different."

Advances in antiretroviral drugs have resolved most of the medical hurdles in treating H.I.V., if not the stigma, according to Marguerita Lightfoot, director of the Center for AIDS Prevention Studies at the University of California, San Francisco.

"In the early days treatment was multiple pills, multiple times a day," she said.

"Often they had to be refrigerated. Some were toxic, they made people sick. So maybe at one time the Army's policy made sense.

"But now it's so easy. And if properly treated, the virus is no longer a risk to the patient or others."

In September, she noted, the Centers for Disease Control and Prevention announced that patients following a proper treatment plan, who have an undetectable level of virus in blood tests, pose "effectively no risk" of transmitting the virus to others.

"I work with doctors and nurses who are H.I.V. positive and there is no risk to patients. I don't see why it would be different in the Army," Dr. Lightfoot said.

Today, policies differ within the military. The Navy allows sailors with H.I.V. to serve on some large ships and overseas bases. The Army does not.

Sergeant Harrison, 41, who now works as a civilian lawyer in the Washington area, grew up in a small town in Oklahoma and enlisted in 2000 as an airborne infantry soldier. After a stint stationed in Alaska, he moved to the National Guard and used his military benefits to attend college, then law school. His schooling was interrupted by deployments to Afghanistan and Kuwait, where he earned medals for good conduct.

In 2012, with a law degree from the University of Oklahoma, he passed the Oklahoma bar exam. The National Guard then offered him a job as an Army lawyer in the Judge Advocate General's Corps.

Around the same time, Sergeant Harrison learned that he had contracted H.I.V. through a sexual partner.

The sergeant was cleared medically to become an officer, and his leaders approved. But because the job would require him to leave his enlisted position and re-enter the Army as an officer, the policy barring new recruits with H.I.V. prohibited the move.

"It makes no sense to me that they say I'm healthy enough to be an infantryman, but not a lawyer," he said.

Sergeant Harrison applied for a medical waiver in 2014, but was denied. He appealed to the Army's head of personnel in 2015, then to the office of the secretary of defense in 2016. Both refused to give him an exception.

The lawsuit filed this week seeks to give the sergeant his commission as a captain and strike down current H.I.V. policies affecting recruiting and deployment across the military.

"Logistically, there is no problem. All my medical exams show I'm in top physical shape. I've had complete support from my units. My commanders signed off on the promotion," Sergeant Harrison said. "But up at the upper levels, the Pentagon, I get the feeling things are a little outdated."

Gender and Sexuality

Historically, the U.S. military has primarily welcomed heterosexual, cisgender men. Even after women began joining, their roles were limited for decades. Gay, lesbian and bisexual soldiers were scrutinized in the early 1990s, as the Clinton administration enacted the "Don't Ask, Don't Tell" policy, which prohibited harassment of soldiers who had not disclosed their sexual orientation, but barred openly homosexual or bisexual soldiers from service. Although the policy was officially ended by the Obama administration in 2011, stigma and discrimination still exist in the military, particularly as the Trump administration has clouded the future of transgender personnel.

Should Women Be Sent Into Combat?

BY DONALD G. MCNEIL JR. | **JULY 21, 1991**

EXPOSURE to danger is not combat. Being shot at, even being killed, is not combat. Combat is finding … closing with … and killing or capturing the enemy. It's KILLING. And it's done in an environment that is often as difficult as you can possibly imagine. Extremes of climate. Brutality. Death. Dying. It's … uncivilized! And women CAN'T DO IT! Nor should they even be thought of as doing it. The requirements for strength and endurance render them UNABLE to do it. And I may be old-fashioned, but I think the very nature of women disqualifies them from doing it. Women give life. Sustain life. Nurture life. They don't TAKE it.

THAT CONGRESSIONAL TESTIMONY last month by Gen. Robert H. Barrow, who retired in 1983 as Commandant of the Marine Corps, suggests what women who want to fight may have to confront first.

General Barrow's presentation was impassioned, but he delivered the same message to the Senate Armed Services Committee as the more rhetorically cautious service chiefs and as two female sergeants, one from the Marines and one from the 82d Airborne: the chiefs don't want women to fight, and many enlisted women don't want to either.

The issue has been raised partly because the war in the gulf — and General Barrow was scoffing at claims that women were baptized in combat there — led to an amendment to a military budget bill that would allow, but not require, the Air Force, Navy and Marines to let women pilots fly combat missions. The Army is governed by policy, not law, but would probably follow suit. The House has passed the bill. The Senate committee voted July 11 to study the amendment further and not vote on it until 1993. If the full Senate agrees, the two houses must work out their differences in conference on the bill this fall.

Defenders of letting women fill combat jobs say the services now hew to a paternalistic and inequitable policy: not keeping service-women from getting killed, but still not letting them kill. They argue that killing is what the military does, meaning the top ranks are nearly closed to those who don't at least learn the trade. If qualified women, they say, are allowed to be surgeons, astronauts and Supreme Court Justices — and military police and instructor pilots — then they ought to be able to lead rifle companies and strafe tank columns.

FIRST BARRIERS ARE IN THE AIR

If the barriers fall, they will do so first in the air, where no heavy lifting is required and some women already train men as combat pilots. Then presumably some combat ships — even the redoubtable Royal Navy has women aboard theirs. Artillery may be next, since missile artil-lery is now open to women, and it is a specialty few men request; only one graduate of the last West Point class did. But other ground combat jobs, where strength and endurance matter in decisions like "Can this platoon carry a 52-pound mortar and enough 5-pound rounds to make it worth carrying?" may wait a long time.

The pressure to open the ranks is coming largely from pilots, most of whom are officers, and there is little clamor from enlisted women. Nor is there a pressing military need. Nor a civilian groundswell.

"I get a letter a day from clergymen saying we ought to change our policy on homosexuals," Michael P. W. Stone, Secretary of the Army, said last week. "I don't get a letter a month saying we ought to change it on women." At the same time, in contrast to General Barrow, he said he thought that physical differences, even for the infantry, were "irrelevant," that the services could "design around the limitations."

But he did not favor easing standards. Basic training has easier tests for women, and women go to parachute school. But they are not allowed in advanced combat training, like Ranger school — considered a "ticket punch" to higher rank even for officers in specialties like intelligence or logistics — where jungle and desert warfare is taught on long sleepless exercises with heavy equipment. Nor do women become SEALs, whose six months of training include 14-mile races by seven-man teams carrying telephone poles and ocean swims while hog-tied.

Since Canada opened its infantry course to women in 1989, under orders from a human rights tribunal, only one of 102 women has passed.

EQUAL OPPORTUNITY

Opening combat to women also raises a thorny civil rights issue. Equal opportunity is not the same in the military as it is in civilian life — where no one actually forces you to, say, take a job or sit at a lunch counter. When pressed, commanders can take any soldier in any specialty, except chaplains and medics, and make him a rifleman. In wartime, infantry units often must be filled that way. If combat jobs are opened to women officers who want them, courts citing the equal protection doctrine would presumably rule that women who don't want them are eligible for transfer too, just as men are.

Two female officers who testified before Senator John Glenn's subcommittee on defense manpower said that risk is part of signing up to defend your country. The two sergeants said many women would think about quitting instead. Recruiters might face a nightmare. The services prize their enlisted women, who have more education, initially get promoted faster, and even when pregnancy leave is included, take less time off than men, who lose it to sports and auto injuries and drug, alcohol and discipline problems.

Proponents of letting women fill some combat jobs recall the aphorisms that were once used to keep blacks out of them, to wit, that they would run, could not follow orders, and were psychologically unequipped to lead whites. Only through integration under Truman did such notions get refuted. Women, they argue, deserve the same chance.

All Combat Roles Now Open to Women, Defense Secretary Says

BY MATTHEW ROSENBERG AND DAVE PHILIPPS | DEC. 3, 2015

IN A HISTORIC transformation of the American military, Defense Secretary Ashton B. Carter said on Thursday that the Pentagon would open all combat jobs to women.

"There will be no exceptions," Mr. Carter said at a news conference. He added, "They'll be allowed to drive tanks, fire mortars and lead infantry soldiers into combat. They'll be able to serve as Army Rangers and Green Berets, Navy SEALs, Marine Corps infantry, Air Force parajumpers and everything else that was previously open only to men."

The groundbreaking decision overturns a longstanding rule that had restricted women from combat roles, even though women have often found themselves in combat in Iraq and Afghanistan over the past 14 years.

It is the latest in a long march of inclusive steps by the military, including racial integration in 1948 and the lifting of the ban on gay men and lesbians serving openly in the military in 2011. The decision this week will open about 220,000 military jobs to women.

The military faced a deadline set by the Obama administration three years ago to integrate women into all combat jobs by January or ask for specific exemptions. The Navy and Air Force have already opened almost all combat positions to women, and the Army has increasingly integrated its forces.

The announcement Thursday was a rebuke to the Marine Corps, which has a 93 percent male force dominated by infantry and a culture that still segregates recruits by gender for basic training. In September, the Marines requested an exemption for infantry and armor positions, citing a yearlong study that showed integration could hurt its fighting ability. But Mr. Carter said he overruled the Marines because the military should operate under a common set of standards.

Gen. Joseph E. Dunford Jr., the former commandant of the Marine Corps who recently became chairman of the Joint Chiefs of Staff, did not attend the announcement, and in a statement Thursday appeared to give only tepid support, saying, "I have had the opportunity to provide my advice on the issue of full integration of women into the armed forces. In the wake of the secretary's decision, my responsibility is to ensure his decision is properly implemented."

Women have long chafed under the combat restrictions, which allowed them to serve in combat zones, often under fire, but prevented them from officially holding combat positions, including in the infantry, which remain crucial to career advancement. Women have long said that by not recognizing their real service, the military has unfairly held them back.

A major barrier fell this year when women were permitted to go through the grueling training that would allow them to qualify as Army Rangers, the service's elite infantry.

Mr. Carter said that women would be allowed to serve in all military combat roles by early next year. He characterized the change as necessary to ensure that the United States military remained the world's most powerful.

"When I became secretary of defense, I made a commitment to building America's force of the future," Mr. Carter told reporters. "In the 21st century that requires drawing strength from the broadest possible pool of talent. This includes women."

Many women hailed the decision. "I'm overjoyed," said Katelyn van Dam, an attack helicopter pilot in the Marine Corps who has deployed to Afghanistan. "Now if there is some little girl who wants to be a tanker, no one can tell her she can't."

But the Republican chairmen of the Senate and House Armed Services Committees expressed caution and noted that by law Congress had 30 days to review the decision.

"Secretary Carter's decision to open all combat positions to women will have a consequential impact on our service members and our

Cpl. Christina Oliver, 25, a United States Marine with the Female Engagement Team, patrolled near an Afghan village to clear the area of Taliban in 2010.

military's warfighting capabilities," Senator John McCain of Arizona and Representative Mac Thornberry of Texas said in a statement. "The Senate and House Armed Services Committees intend to carefully and thoroughly review all relevant documentation related to today's decision."

Some in the military have privately voiced concern that integration will prove impractical, especially in the infantry, where heavy loads and long periods of deprivation are part of the job.

"Humping a hundred pounds, man, that ain't easy, and it remains the defining physical requirement of the infantry," said Paul Davis, an exercise scientist who did a multiyear study of the Marine infantry. "The practical reality is that even though we want to knock down this last bastion of exclusion, the preponderance of women will not be able to do the job."

Mr. Carter acknowledged at the news conference that simply opening up combat roles to women was not going to lead to a fully integrated military. Senior defense officials and military officers would have to overcome the perception among many service members, men and women alike, that the change would reduce the effectiveness of the armed services.

The defense secretary sought to assuage those concerns on Thursday by saying that every service member would have to meet the standards of the jobs they wished to fill, and "there must be no quotas or perception thereof."

He also acknowledged that many units were likely to remain largely male, especially elite infantry troops and Special Operations forces, where "only small numbers of women could" likely meet the standards.

"Studies say there are physical differences," Mr. Carter said, though he added that some women could meet the most demanding physical requirements, just as some men could not.

At the same time, he said, military leaders are going to be required to assign jobs and tasks and determine who is promoted based on "ability, not gender."

Lt. Col. Kate Germano, who oversaw the training of female recruits for the Marines until she was removed this summer from duty during a dispute over what she said were lower standards for women in basic training, said by creating standards, the military would improve across both genders.

She said while Marines have long resisted the idea of women in combat units, she did not expect a backlash.

"One thing about the Marine Corps, once you tell us what we have to do, we'll do it," she said. "There was resistance to lifting the ban on gays, too, and when it was lifted there were no issues. We are a stronger force for it."

Mr. Carter's announcement came less than a month from the three-year deadline set by the Obama administration to integrate the force.

Some veterans of recent wars say the unexpectedly long period of combat with no clear enemy lines may have been a driver for the change.

"I honestly didn't think about women in combat much until Iraq," said Jonathan Silk, a retired Army major who served in Afghanistan and Iraq as a cavalry scout.

In the fray of the insurgency, he said, integrated military police units near him often faced ferocious attacks. "That is where I encountered female soldiers that were in the same firefights as us, facing the same horrible stuff, even if they weren't technically in combat units. They could fight just as well as I could, and some of those women were tremendous leaders. It gave me such respect."

The Thickest Glass Ceiling
in the Marine Corps Breaks

OPINION | BY TERESA FAZIO | SEPT. 25, 2017

IT IS A RITE OF PASSAGE that I have experienced: brand-new lieutenants introducing themselves to their platoons of a few dozen enlisted
Marines. It is a powerful experience for any new officer. Now consider
the stakes when that lieutenant is a woman — and the platoon is a front-
line infantry unit. The Marine Corps is the most male-dominated of the
armed services, and the infantry is the most male-dominated bastion
of the corps. The moment will be electric, and historic.

Soon enough it will also be a reality. On Monday, the Marine Corps
graduated the first woman ever from its famously grueling Infantry Officer Course. (The Marine Corps has withheld the lieutenant's
name, at her request.) Of 36 women who have attempted the course
since 2012, she is the sole finisher. I recall driving down Quantico roads
and passing filthy, sweat-drenched former classmates from the Basic
School (the gender-integrated, six-month course for new lieutenants
from all parts of the corps) going through the Infantry Officer Course.
They carried weapons and heavy packs, and one time, were red-faced
and sputtering from being tear-gassed without masks. About a quarter
of all applicants, almost all of them men, fail, 10 percent on the first day.

Infantry is the hallowed "tip of the spear" for the Marine Corps,
among the first combatants into war zones. In keeping with the ethos
of "every Marine a rifleman," all Marines learn basic infantry skills,
but only about 19 percent of the Corps is actually infantry; a few percent more encompass other combat arms specialties like artillery
and armored vehicles. The rest of the corps supports them, whether
through logistics, communications or gunfire from the air. Only since
early 2016 have combat arms occupational specialties — including the
infantry — been open to women. Women have made it into the infantry
as enlisted Marines, but until now, none have become infantry officers.

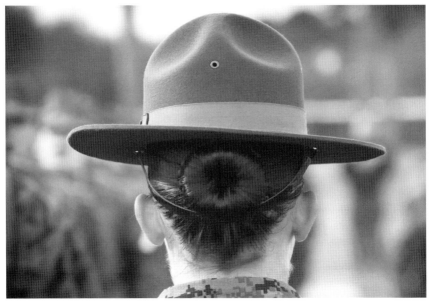

A Marine drill instructor in South Carolina. The first woman has just graduated from the Marine Corps' grueling infantry officer course.

Gender integration in the combat arms has been a source of much passionate debate within the military. About a year ago, the Pentagon released the results of a 2012 study by the think tank CNA that found that 76.5 percent of male Marines who have served in ground combat units were opposed to women in combat arms (56.4 percent of noncombat male Marines were, too). But this study was done at least three years before there were widespread integration efforts, including the corps' Ground Combat Element Integrated Task Force, a unit created to study gender integration. None of the infantrymen had ever seen female Marines meeting the same physical standards as them. Now they have.

Similar concerns about unit cohesion were also debated in the wake of the reversal of the "don't ask, don't tell" policy on gay troops. Before the policy change, 59.4 percent of Marines who had been deployed in combat believed that allowing homosexuals to serve openly would hurt unit effectiveness. But one year after the change, a Palm Center study found no impact on military readiness, unit cohesion, recruitment or retention. Moreover, studies from RAND have found that the "performance of a group influences its cohesion more than cohesion influences performance."

But no number of facts, stats and averages can prepare someone for the actual experience of serving on the front lines. By integrating only women who have already met the infantry's difficult training standards, the corps acknowledges that military readiness is paramount. At the end of the day, this newly minted infantry officer will prove herself by the way she carries herself around her fellow Marines. Peer leadership, too, will be important. Her classmates have seen her perform and can be powerful allies as she integrates into the operating forces. As Eleanor Taylor, the first female Canadian infantry company commander, said in 2013, "Initial infantry training is a crucible." She continued, "If the training is properly executed and she is successful, she will earn fierce loyalty from her peers and will be fully integrated into the team."

At the same time, this female officer can be a key tactical asset to her unit if they deploy to Afghanistan, where Marines have returned this year. Female troops are invaluable for searching houses and communicating with local women, gaining access to spaces and information that, because of local custom, male troops cannot get. Her integration can expand her unit's capabilities and help save lives.

What remains to be seen is how readily she will be accepted at the small-unit level, rife with locker-room shoving, wrestling and pornography — all of which, since she's made it this far, she's most likely seen already. The first few training exercises she does with her troops will show them her strength and, ideally, garner the support of small-unit leaders who will back her up. Through pulling heavy cables, throwing down one another in martial arts training and running in 115-degree Iraqi heat, my senior enlisted Marines helped me become the officer I was. They offered suggestions, but reminded me that command presence comes from within oneself.

Top-down, the Marine Corps brass continues to look for ways to battle undercurrents of misogyny, especially in the wake of the Marines United nude photo-sharing scandal this spring. At the same time, the Marines United perpetrators were not solely infantrymen; a great many served in noncombat units. Bigotry and misogyny know no occupational specialty, neither in the Marine Corps nor in the world outside. Since leaving the corps, I've earned a Ph.D. in materials science and worked in technology — fields for which women, just decades ago, were deemed unfit. Though it is a long road to eliminating workplace sexism and harassment, we are at a hinge point in history when it comes to gender integration; the infantry is just the latest field to open up.

In that vein, the corps is developing professional military education; leadership is convening focus groups of active-duty Marines to examine gender bias and social cohesion. Proactively acknowledging preconceived ideas about gender in small-group discussions can be productive. Sgt. Danielle Beck, who participated in the 2015 Ground Combat Element Integrated Task Force as an antitank missileman, said, "We got to a point where we all talked about it openly, and no one was mad about it; we just talked professionally."

I anticipate there will be little fanfare from the Marine Corps regarding the graduation. As The Times has noted, the Army's graduation ceremony for its first female infantry soldiers made no mention that some of them were women — and that is as it should be. Monday's graduation is important because it paves the way for women in combat arms *not to* be a big deal in the future. Like her male classmates, this officer has met an exceptionally high standard. Soon, she will be just one more Marine infantry lieutenant, picking up her first platoon.

TERESA FAZIO, a former Marine captain, served from 2002 until 2006 and was deployed to Iraq with a communications unit in 2004.

Military Women, Too, Should Serve Unmolested

OPINION | BY SUPRIYA VENKATESAN | OCT. 18, 2017

IT WAS 2004 and I had been in the Army for only three months when I first began to suspect something was wrong. I was walking by our drill sergeant's desk, where he sat, leaning back in his chair. On the floor in front of him was a newly arrived female soldier. She was on her back, dressed in T-shirt and shorts, doing scissor kicks. He sat perfectly poised to see her crotch and the insides of her thighs.

In one sense, this wasn't unusual. In Advanced Individual Training, soldiers are drilled in technical skills after Combat Basic Training. Here we get "smoked" — we are given grueling punishments designed to build us up physically and break us down mentally so that we can be whip-shaped into soldiers who do exactly as told. The soldier on her back was doing exactly as told.

I was in the same class as this woman at Fort Gordon, a military installation set among the world-famous golf courses of Augusta, Ga. The drill sergeant had a reputation of "smoking out" women with flutter kicks and other sexually driven punishments, but at the time, I viewed my drill sergeants with great reverence. It seemed then to be something rare, something I would never see again in the military. I was wrong.

A few months later, at my first duty station at Camp Hovey in South Korea, my platoon sergeant told me very directly that all female soldiers were "lazy sluts" and that I was going to become one too. He explained to me that the military was undergoing a uniform change, not to allow us to mesh into the desert and urban jungles of emerging combat environments but because more women were joining the military and we were all "dirty whores."

After months of daily berating from my platoon sergeant, I finally mustered the courage to tell my 1st sergeant, the senior enlisted leader at my company. He listened without much response and the next day moved me to another platoon. I was grateful, but I also noticed that no action was taken against the platoon sergeant. Because soldiers generally get moved because of misconduct, rumors began to spread about me. As is often the case with harassment or assault, I, the victim, was shamed.

In an impassioned statement at a Senate Armed Services Committee hearing earlier this year, Senator Kirsten Gillibrand said, "We know from reports 60 percent of men and 58 percent of women who experience sexual harassment or gender discrimination indicated a supervisor was one of the people engaged in the violations. That is a problem with our command." My own experience and those I've learned about from other women support this statistic.

I witnessed misogyny at all levels of my six years in the military. On Monday mornings, while working in the motor pool to clean and maintain our Humvees, male soldiers would gather around a single cellphone to watch porn and talk in detail of their sexual escapades. I quickly learned and got accustomed to hearing terms for violent sexual activity too graphic to detail here. This language and the images of sexual violence they represented quickly became part of my psychological reality. I myself began to objectify women, and found myself troubled and confused by my own gender identity.

Misogyny was present in the smallest of things, like the nude pin-ups of women that the chain of command allowed in work shelters, but bigger things, too, like the frequent accounts of male-on-female assault and rape. One of my friends, on a deployment to Afghanistan, was so brutally raped by a male soldier that she is now physically unable to carry and give birth to a child. (She was recently medically discharged after 19 years of active duty and is in rehabilitation for post-traumatic stress disorder, including daily thoughts of suicide.) Another friend, while stationed in South Korea, was tied up in her bedroom, raped and beaten by several male soldiers, then found in a bloody bath four days later.

In the United States, sexual assault is reported to be declining (dropping 58 percent between 1995 and 2010). But in the military it's increasing enormously, so much so that the United Nations has gotten involved and the Pentagon reported that the military received a record number of sexual assault reports in 2016. This year we saw the persistence of this culture in the Marines United photo scandal, in which hundreds of Marines circulated intimate photos of women to a secret Facebook group without their consent. Despite the historical advances of women into combat and leadership roles, not a whole lot is being done to change this culture.

Misogyny, of course, is present in every other sector of society, but there is an important distinction in the military. Michael Kimmel, author of "Angry White Men" and a professor of sociology at Stony Brook University, told me, "The military is the same as every other organization, in that these informal cultural barriers have shown up everywhere." But the military is different because of transparent hierarchy. "If the top of the military wanted this to stop, it would stop. Period."

The military, more than any other American institution, runs on an unwavering chain of command. It is entirely based on the taking and giving of orders. But there remain entrenched problems with the system of military justice. It is the chain of command that is responsible for investigation and punishment of sexual assaults.

In 2013, Senator Gillibrand introduced legislation to remove the chain of command from handling these cases. It narrowly failed to meet the 60-vote threshold required to avoid a filibuster. In 2014, Senator Gillibrand fought and lost again. In 2016, she tried to reintroduce the bill, but the Republican leadership would not allow the bill onto the floor because the Department of Defense said taking away commanders' authority would "undermine good order and discipline." As a result, reports from the department's Sexual Assault Prevention and Response Office show that year after year, almost no progress has been made toward ending sexual assault in the military, despite its repeated promises to do so.

Lawrence Korb, a former assistant secretary of defense and senior fellow at the Center for American Progress, told me, "The chain of command cannot be involved in issues of sexual assault because the issue gets diluted and distorted." A military lawyer I deployed with agrees. He estimated that in his eight years of service, "95 percent of crimes prosecuted were crimes caught, or reported, by an outside agency, not internal to the unit." This was because those crimes being reported by an outside agency had to be prosecuted. Otherwise, commanders would bury allegations because having harassment or assault cases reflects poorly on them. As a manager, it's simply easier to squash the problem by transferring the accused perpetrator or the victim out of the unit.

Many of our closest allies' militaries, including those of Britain, Canada, Israel, Germany, Norway and Australia, have already moved reporting and prosecution of violent sex crimes outside of the chain of command. But why haven't we?

Some in the military have decided on their own that it will stop, with them.

When I was moved into a different platoon in South Korea, I fell under the leadership of the man who would become my mentor. With his guidance, I pushed myself physically, getting near-perfect scores on my fitness and marksmanship tests. He helped me study for Soldier of the Month competitions, which I won numerous times. This led to my promotion to sergeant, just shy of my second anniversary of being in the Army. When rumors spread that I was promoted because I must have slept around, my mentor sat down with the rest of my platoon and set them straight. He told them forcefully that it was not true and to cease the rumor spreading immediately.

Because someone defended me at that critical moment, and because of guidance from other true leaders, I was able to sharpen my mental and physical acumen and attain positions in the United States Embassy in Iraq and as a member of the personal staff for Lt. Gen. Frank Helmick, the former commanding general of the XVIII Airborne Corps. General Helmick nurtured my passion for writing and planted the seed for me to later pursue it professionally. These positive experiences with men greatly enhanced my self-worth and have helped me succeed, both in and out of the military.

I wish I could say my military career ended well, but it didn't. As my career progressed, I was confronted with more poor treatment by my superiors. It became all too clear to me that despite the many devoted, professional men who hold up the honor of military service, the atmosphere toward women in general had not changed.

The military is morally obligated to stop the systemwide mistreatment of women in its ranks, but that change will not be made until it is enforced from the top leadership on down. It is too big and important a job to be left to a few good men.

SUPRIYA VENKATESAN (@supriya_venk) is an Army veteran and a freelance writer. She is at work on a book about her experiences in the military.

Reports of Sexual Assault in the Military Rise by 10 Percent, Pentagon Finds

BY THOMAS GIBBONS-NEFF | APRIL 30, 2018

WASHINGTON — More than 6,700 Defense Department employees reported being sexually assaulted in the 2017 fiscal year — the highest number since the United States military began tracking reports more than a decade ago, according to Pentagon data released on Monday.

The new data showed a 10 percent increase of military sexual assault reports from the previous fiscal year. The uptick occurred amid a Marine Corps scandal over sharing nude photos and heightened public discourse about sexual harassment in American culture. Pentagon officials sought to portray the increase as reflective of more troops and military civilians trusting commanders and the military's judicial system enough to come forward.

In all, 6,769 people reported assaults for the 2017 fiscal year, which ended Sept. 30. It was the largest yearly increase since 2014 and the most reports since the Pentagon started tracking the data in 2006.

Roughly two-thirds of the reports resulted in disciplinary action, the data show. The remaining 38 percent were discounted because evidence was lacking, victims declined to participate in hearings or other reasons.

The Army, Navy and Air Force each saw a roughly 10 percent uptick in sexual assault reports. The increase nearly reached 15 percent in the Marine Corps.

Separately, roughly 700 complaints of sexual harassment were reported across the military in the 2017 fiscal year, according to the Pentagon data. Ninety percent of the reports were from enlisted troops.

In March 2017, a social media group made up of active duty and former Marines was accused of sharing explicit photos of female colleagues, prompting a widespread investigation by the Naval Criminal Investigative Service. A number of Marines were punished, and the service started a campaign to educate its troops on sexual harassment and assault.

Despite efforts to rid the internet of military-themed groups such as the one found last year, others have continued to pop up.

Gen. Robert B. Neller, the Marine Corps commandant, said the service was in a "better place" after the scandal.

Lawmakers have long hammered the military on its predominantly male culture and have sometimes lobbied for military courts to be civilian run so due process is absent of command influence.

Defense Secretary Jim Mattis, who last week called sexual assault a "cancer" in the military, has demanded that leaders throughout the ranks make sure the problem does not spread.

From Annapolis to Congress? These Three Women Know Tough Missions

BY MICHAEL TACKETT | JAN. 29, 2018

NORFOLK, VA. — Elaine Luria commanded an assault ship with a crew of 400 that patrolled the Persian Gulf for hostile Iranian vessels. Amy McGrath was the first female Marine to fly in an F-18 fighter jet in combat, dropping bombs over Afghanistan and Iraq. Mikie Sherrill was certified as a Navy helicopter pilot only after passing an underwater crash simulation in which she was blindfolded, turned upside down, and forced to find the sole exit door.

Their military journeys began at the United States Naval Academy, where Ms. Luria and Ms. McGrath were plebes together when Ms. Sherrill was a senior. Now they are on a mission that no female Annapolis graduate has accomplished: to win seats in Congress.

A powerful wave of political activism is animating women in the era of President Trump, stoked by women's marches and the movement to expose sexual misconduct. More than 390 women are running for Congress, a record number, and they are overwhelmingly Democrats.

But the three Naval Academy graduates, all Democrats themselves, are offering something that breaks through — the kind of military credentials and academy service that have propelled men to office since the founding of the country. And they are running in swing districts where military service is likely to resonate and where Democrats must win to wrest control of the House from Republicans.

"It's incredibly important that I decided to serve my country before deciding to run for office," said Ms. Sherrill, whose path to the House became easier on Monday when her Republican opponent, Representative Rodney Frelinghuysen, chairman of the House Appropriations Committee, announced his retirement. "That shows where my center is." Strategists in both parties say that women — as candidates, activists and voters — are more likely to shape the outcome of the midterm elections than any other part of the electorate.

Republicans have their own female veterans running for House seats: Aja Smith in inland Southern California and Lynne Blankenbeker in New Hampshire. Representative Martha McSally, Republican of Arizona and an Air Force Academy graduate and decorated fighter pilot, is running for the Senate.

But Democrats have the trickier task — flipping enough seats in often gerrymandered Republican districts to take the House. Ms. Luria is running in the Tidewater Region of Virginia, home to the world's largest naval base and the headquarters of the Christian Broadcasting Network. If she wins her primary race, she is likely to face Representative Scott Taylor, a freshman Republican with his own military credential, as a Navy SEAL.

The district where Ms. McGrath is running in Kentucky sprawls across 19 rural and urban counties that include Lexington. But her contest, even with her compelling background, might be the toughest of the three. Many Democrats in Washington prefer her primary opponent, Jim Gray, the mayor of Lexington, who is better known and can fund much of the race with his own money.

Ms. McGrath has gained a measure of celebrity with an initial campaign video highlighting her military experience and her criticism of Mr. Trump. It has attracted more than one million page views and, more important, generated more than $1 million in campaign contributions.

The New Jersey district that Ms. Sherrill is running in went for Mr. Trump by less than a percentage point, then voted for the new Democratic governor, Phil Murphy.

All three women lean heavily on their military backgrounds to promote their campaigns, with photos in uniform dominating their websites. But they also share the challenges of any first-time candidate: raising money, building an organization and avoiding rookie mistakes.

Seated at a table in the Norfolk business she started while still on active duty, Mermaid Factory, where customers paint molds of mermaids, Ms. Luria noted how important ties to the Navy were in her district, which includes the state's largest city, Virginia Beach. She served for 20 years before retiring last June, and decided only a few months later to run for Congress.

Ms. Luria said that she felt the pull to run for office after Mr. Trump's election, and that her husband quit his job to help take over household duties so she could focus on campaigning.

She grew up in Birmingham, Ala., where her family owned a scrap metal business. She was drawn to two seemingly contradictory passions — art and engineering — which she thought she could pursue at the Naval Academy.

"I went to Annapolis and was really just brainwashed," she said. "The midshipmen seemed like they knew everything in the world. I wanted to be just like them."

Unlike many at the academy, she was not particularly athletic. But she had earned a black belt in taekwondo, passed all the required endurance tests and flourished in the classroom. She also mastered the required manner of eating for plebes, squaring her bites and taking no more than three chews before swallowing.

She decided on surface warfare and rose to become a commander.

"A ship is like a city at sea," she said. "The junior sailor cleaning the head is as important as the officer on the radar scope."

After the Sept. 11 terrorist attacks, she said, she felt compelled to stay in the Navy. She had a letter of resignation stuck in her desk, but never submitted it.

Women in public opinion polls have been more critical of Mr. Trump than men, and they have used elections to cast a vote against him, most notably in recent races in Virginia. But Ms. Luria said that she would rather focus on policy disagreements than the president's behavior.

All three women said they were drawn to the idea of public office from their first days at the academy, when they had to memorize a mission statement that said they would dedicate themselves to both citizenship and leadership.

The district in Kentucky that Amy McGrath, right, is running to represent sprawls across 19 rural and urban counties that include Lexington.

The Navy exposed them to Americans, and immigrants, from all walks of life, they said, and that has helped as they campaign in their diverse districts.

While Ms. Luria has institutional party support, Ms. McGrath does not. Boisterous, outgoing and quick with an opinion, Ms. McGrath was highly critical of the Democratic Congressional Campaign Committee for encouraging Mr. Gray to enter the race.

"Not only did they not embrace me, they were not even neutral," Ms. McGrath said. "All I wanted them to do was to just stay out of it."

But she has a history of not shying from a fight. Her older brother, Matt, pushed her to compete with boys in every sport, including football.

As an 11-year-old, she became enthralled with fighter pilots after watching a documentary on the History Channel and asked her mother how she could become one. Her mother told her the law prohibited it.

The young girl asked how laws could be changed. She persisted, writing Jim Bunning, her representative in Congress at the time, to ask why women were not allowed to be fighter pilots. Mr. Bunning, who died last May, replied that women were not prohibited because they were considered "inferior," but rather "were perceived as a precious commodity of the country that deserved protection."

"Here I was beating all the boys, and I just did not understand because my name was Amy and not Andy that I couldn't be a jet pilot," Ms. McGrath said.

So she wrote to the members of the congressional armed services committees, and only Patricia Schroeder, then a Democratic congresswoman from Colorado, supported her position.

Then came the election of Bill Clinton in 1992, and Democrats eventually pushed through the kind of change that Ms. McGrath had been seeking.

"That was my first understanding of the difference between Democrats and Republicans," she said. "I knew all the Democrats were willing to give me an opportunity to compete, and the Republicans said no."

She applied to the Naval Academy because she thought that was where the best pilots trained. Ms. McGrath said she loved the atmosphere from the first day — the tougher the better. Soon after graduation, she was flying an F-18.

"The F-18 is the most intense job in the world," she said. "Imagine playing a soccer game and doing math problems and doing a talk radio show at the same time. It completely physically and mentally absorbs everything that you have."

She flew missions in Afghanistan and Iraq, and then did a tour at the Pentagon and as a fellow in Congress. She turned down a possible promotion to have the second of her three children, and earned a master's degree in international relations from Johns Hopkins. After that, she taught at the Naval Academy, and a guest speaker one day was Ben Chandler, a former Congressman from her home state of Kentucky. He gave her his card and asked her to call if she ever needed anything.

"It's incredibly important that I decided to serve my country before deciding to run for office," said Mikie Sherrill, who is running for Congress in New Jersey. "That shows where my center is."

Forty-eight hours after Mr. Trump's election, Ms. McGrath was rummaging through a drawer to find Mr. Chandler's card. She quickly wrote him an emotional email.

"I never really thought I'd ever write you to ask you for some guidance but this week has left me numb," she wrote. "I'm so taken back by who our nation elected president and what he stands for that I feel as if I must do something. I've spent my entire adult life in the service of this country, three combat tours, and literally years of my life living in tents overseas. I love this country, but I've never been more ashamed and embarrassed to be an American as I was waking up on Weds morning."

She wanted to run for Congress. Mr. Chandler put her in touch with his former campaign manager, and she was off.

"I am deeply disappointed in the president," she said. "His character, almost everything he has done in his life and stood for in his life is against everything that I have tried to stand for and do."

If Ms. McGrath is to win her primary race, it appears likely that she will have to do it as an insurgent.

Ms. Sherrill does not have that burden. With the strong backing of her party, she is favored to win her primary and her chances for winning the seat increase with Mr. Frelinghuysen's retirement announcement. She does not speak of Mr. Trump with the sharp edges of Ms. McGrath, focusing her criticism instead on the new tax law and the president's effort to weaken the Affordable Care Act.

Her district is a suburban-exurban blend of mainly prosperous New Jersey suburbs. But like many suburban women, she said she was simply "fed up" with the president's agenda. "I talked to friends and thought if we broke through our own glass ceilings, we would progress, yet we now see again and again we simply haven't made the gains we thought we made. My children's future is in peril."

In addition to her Navy service, Ms. Sherrill was a federal prosecutor, and fretted that it now felt like "our institutions of democracy are under attack."

Gay Soldiers, Good Soldiers

EDITORIAL | BY THE NEW YORK TIMES | SEPT. 1, 1991

DO HOMOSEXUAL PERSONNEL, male and female, threaten the effectiveness of the armed forces? Or is it shortsighted prejudice for the military services to ban homosexuals and to discharge those discovered in its ranks?

That long-festering issue has emerged with new force in recent weeks, requiring Defense Secretary Cheney to explain anew to Congress and the public just why homosexuals are deemed "incompatible with military service."

Mr. Cheney showed little appetite for the task, with good reason. The ban deprives the armed forces of talent and the discharges damage thousands of careers and lives. All for a policy with not a shred of hard evidence to support it.

Much of the opposition to homosexuals reflects a deep-seated fear that gay personnel would make sexual advances on their heterosexual comrades, provoking fights or starting affairs that would destroy discipline. But that wrongly brands all homosexuals as sexual aggressors. The same specter of unrestrained sexuality was raised when women were first admitted to military service. Yet women have been successfully accommodated, and they performed valiantly in the Persian Gulf war.

The Defense Department is actually two-faced on the subject of homosexuality. Homosexuals are allowed to serve in civilian jobs, even at the highest and most sensitive levels, under civil service rules that outlaw sexual orientation as a criterion for employment. That is why Secretary Cheney has no trouble retaining a trusted aide who was identified as homosexual by a gay magazine.

But the department bans homosexuals from military service and has discharged more than 13,000 people as homosexuals since 1982. Many, sad to say, have been outstanding. Some have won bronze or silver stars. One was a naval cadet near the top of his class at Annapolis. Underscoring the absurdity of the policy, the commander of the surface fleet in the Atlantic last year urged, in a message to his subordinates, that investigations of lesbians not be "pursued halfheartedly" just because lesbians are generally "hard-working, career-oriented, willing to put in long hours on the job and among the command's top performers."

The official justification for the ban is a single sweeping paragraph in the Defense Department's administrative discharge directive. It asserts, with dubious accuracy, that the presence of homosexuals "seriously impairs the accomplishment of the military mission" in seven areas, including morale and recruitment.

The Pentagon may be retreating from one claim — that homosexuals are a security risk, peculiarly subject to blackmail. Unpublished studies for the military in 1957 and 1988 concluded that homosexuals were a negligible security risk, and Secretary Cheney dismissed the allegation as "a bit of an old chestnut."

Other assertions that the presence of homosexuals makes it difficult to maintain morale and insure the integrity of the command system sound like worst-case projections based on outdated stereotypes. Polls show that most Americans think homosexuals should be allowed in the military.

The most emotional reason for excluding homosexuals is that service members, in contrast to civilians in the Defense Department, "frequently must live and work under close conditions affording minimal privacy." Perhaps some heterosexual servicemen fear they would be propositioned in the showers. But that possibility could be managed with regulations proscribing sexual harassment. And what consenting adults do on their own time is their business, not the military's.

The military and its civilian overseers need to reexamine the case; there's no evident justification for discrimination on the basis of sexual orientation.

'Don't Ask, Don't Tell'
Is Challenged in Suit

SPECIAL TO THE NEW YORK TIMES | MARCH 8, 1994

WASHINGTON, MARCH 7 — Two civil rights groups today filed the first legal challenge to the Pentagon's new policy and regulations governing homosexuals in the military.

The American Civil Liberties Union and the Lambda Legal Defense and Education Fund filed suit in the United States District Court for the Eastern District of New York on behalf of two service members on active duty and four in the reserves, who are all homosexual.

Under the Clinton Administration's policy characterized as "don't ask, don't tell, don't pursue," gay men and lesbians are allowed to serve in the armed forces so long as they keep their sexual orientation private. The military service branches last week announced specific regulations putting the policy into effect. The lawsuit contends these restrictions infringe on the rights of homosexual members of the military.

Judge Eugene H. Nickerson, who was appointed to the Federal Court in Brooklyn by President Jimmy Carter, is scheduled to hear arguments on March 18 on whether the Pentagon should be ordered to suspend enforcement of its new policy, at least in the case of the six service members in the suit.

Gay rights groups say there is a possibility that Judge Nickerson could issue a broader preliminary injunction, barring the Pentagon from enforcing the policy and regulations on any service member until the case is resolved.

Trump Says Transgender People Will Not Be Allowed in the Military

BY JULIE HIRSCHFELD DAVIS AND HELENE COOPER | JULY 26, 2017

WASHINGTON — President Trump abruptly announced a ban on transgender people serving in the military on Wednesday, blindsiding his defense secretary and Republican congressional leaders with a snap decision that reversed a year-old policy reviled by social conservatives.

Mr. Trump made the declaration on Twitter, saying that American forces could not afford the "tremendous medical costs and disruption" of transgender service members. He said he had consulted generals and military experts, but Jim Mattis, the defense secretary, was given only a day's notice about the decision.

Mr. Trump elected to announce the ban in order to resolve a quietly brewing fight on Capitol Hill over whether taxpayer money should pay for gender transition and hormone therapy for transgender service members. The dispute had threatened to kill a $790 billion defense and security spending package scheduled for a vote this week.

But rather than addressing that narrow issue, Mr. Trump opted to upend the entire policy on transgender service members.

His decision was announced with such haste that the White House could not answer basic inquiries about how it would be carried out, including what would happen to openly transgender people on active duty. Of eight defense officials interviewed, none could say.

"That's something that the Department of Defense and the White House will have to work together as implementation takes place and is done so lawfully," Sarah Huckabee Sanders, the White House press secretary, said.

Still, the announcement pleased elements of Mr. Trump's base who have been dismayed to see the president break so bitterly in recent days with Attorney General Jeff Sessions, a hard-line conservative.

Civil rights and transgender advocacy groups denounced the

policy, with some vowing to challenge it in court. Pentagon officials expressed dismay that the president's tweets could open them to lawsuits.

The ban would reverse the gradual transformation of the military under President Barack Obama, whose administration announced last year that transgender people could serve openly in the military. Mr. Obama's defense secretary, Ashton B. Carter, also opened all combat roles to women and appointed the first openly gay Army secretary.

And it represented a stark turnabout for Mr. Trump, who billed himself during the campaign as an ally of gay, lesbian, bisexual and transgender people.

The president, Ms. Sanders said, had concluded that allowing transgender people to serve openly "erodes military readiness and unit cohesion, and made the decision based on that."

Mr. Mattis, who was on vacation, was silent on the new policy. People close to the defense secretary said he was appalled that Mr. Trump chose to unveil his decision in tweets, in part because of the message they sent to transgender active-duty service members, including those deployed overseas, that they were suddenly no longer welcome.

The policy would affect only a small portion of the approximately 1.3 million active-duty members of the military. Some 2,000 to 11,000 active-duty troops are transgender, according to a 2016 RAND Corporation study commissioned by the Pentagon, though estimates of the number of transgender service members have varied widely, and are sometimes as high as 15,000.

The study found that allowing transgender people to serve openly in the military would "have minimal impact on readiness and health care costs" for the Pentagon. It estimated that health care costs would rise $2.4 million to $8.4 million a year, representing an infinitesimal 0.04 to 0.13 percent increase in spending. Citing research into other countries that allow transgender people to serve, the study projected "little or no impact on unit cohesion, operational effectiveness or readiness" in the United States.

Lt. Commander Blake Dremann, a Navy supply corps officer who is transgender, said he found out his job was in danger when he turned on CNN on Wednesday morning. Commander Dremann came out as transgender to his commanders in 2015, and said they had been supportive of him.

He refused to criticize Mr. Trump — "we don't criticize our commander in chief," he said — but said the policy shift "is singling out a specific population in the military, who had been assured we were doing everything appropriate to continue our honorable service."

He added: "And I will continue to do so, until the military tells me to hang up my boots."

The announcement came amid the debate on Capitol Hill over the Obama-era practice of requiring the Pentagon to pay for medical treatment related to gender transition. Representative Vicky Hartzler, Republican of Missouri, has proposed an amendment to the spending bill that would bar the Pentagon from spending money on transition surgery or related hormone therapy, and other Republicans have pressed for similar provisions.

Mr. Mattis had worked behind the scenes to keep such language out of legislation, quietly lobbying Republican lawmakers not to attach the prohibitions, according to congressional and defense officials.

But Mr. Trump was concerned that the transgender medical care issue could imperil the security spending measure, which also contains $1.6 billion for the border wall that he has championed, and wanted to resolve the dispute cleanly and straightforwardly, according to a person familiar with his thinking, who insisted on anonymity to describe it. That prompted his ban.

Republican congressional leaders were aware Mr. Trump was looking into whether taxpayer money should be spent on medical procedures for transgender service members, but had not expected him to go so far as to bar transgender people from serving altogether.

Mr. Trump and Republican lawmakers had come under pressure from Tony Perkins, the president of the Family Research Council, a leading Christian conservative group, and an ally of Mr. Trump's. Mr. Perkins opposed the bill over spending on transgender medical costs and lobbied lawmakers to do the same.

"Grant repentance to President Trump and Secretary Mattis for even considering to keep this wicked policy in place," the Family Research Council said in one of its daily prayers last week. "Grant them understanding, courage and willpower to stand up to the forces of darkness that gave birth to it and wholly to repeal it."

Opponents of allowing openly transgender service members had raised a number of concerns, including what they said was the questionable psychological fitness of those troops. They said the military was being used for social experimentation at the expense of national security.

"This was Ash Carter on his way out the door pulling the pin on a cultural grenade," Mr. Perkins said on Wednesday. "Our military leaders are saying this doesn't help make us a better fighting force; it's a distraction; it's taking up limited resources."

Mr. Carter objected to the decision, for its effect on the military and on those considering joining.

"To choose service members on other grounds than military qualifications is social policy and has no place in our military," he said in a statement. "There are already transgender individuals who are serving capably and honorably. This action would also send the wrong signal to a younger generation thinking about military service."

While some conservative lawmakers, including Ms. Hartzler, praised Mr. Trump, the president drew bipartisan condemnation on Capitol Hill and outrage from civil rights and transgender advocacy groups.

"There is no reason to force service members who are able to fight, train and deploy to leave the military — regardless of their gender identity," said Senator John McCain, Republican of Arizona and the chairman of the Senate Armed Services Committee.

He called Mr. Trump's move "yet another example of why major policy announcements should not be made via Twitter."

Senator Jack Reed, Democrat of Rhode Island and the ranking member of the Armed Services Committee, noted the irony of Mr. Trump's announcing the ban on the anniversary of President Harry Truman's order to desegregate the military. "President Trump is choosing to retreat in the march toward equality," he said.

In June, the administration delayed by six months a decision on whether to allow transgender recruits to join the military. At the time, Mr. Mattis said the delay would give military leaders a chance to review the shift's potential impact. Mr. Mattis's decision was seen as a pause to "finesse" the issue, one official said, not a prelude to an outright ban.

The delay on recruits "was largely based on a disagreement on the science of how mental health care and hormone therapy for transgender individuals would help solve the medical issues that are associated with gender dysphoria," Gen. Paul Selva, the vice chairman of the Joint Chiefs of Staff, said during his reconfirmation hearing last week.

"I am an advocate of every qualified person who can meet the physical standards to serve in our uniformed services to be able to do so," he said.

Mr. Mattis, a retired Marine, has not been a major proponent of allowing transgender people to serve in the military, in part because medical accommodations, including hormone injections, could open the Defense Department to claims from other people not allowed to serve, like Type 1 diabetics, who also need regular injections.

But Mr. Mattis and the Pentagon's military leadership all seemed to have accepted that transgender people already serving in the military would be allowed to remain. A senior adviser to Mr. Mattis, Sally Donnelly, represented the Palm Center, an organization that advocated on behalf of the L.G.B.T. community in the military during the debate that led up to the Obama administration's decision to allow transgender people to serve, defense officials said.

Mr. Trump's abrupt decision is likely to end up in court; OutServe-SLDN, a nonprofit group that represents gay, lesbian, bisexual and transgender people in the military, immediately vowed to sue.

"We have transgender individuals who serve in elite SEAL teams, who are working in a time of war to defend our country, and now you're going to kick them out?" Matthew F. Thorn, executive director of Out-Serve, said in an interview.

For Transgender Service Members, a Mix of Sadness, Anger and Fear

BY DAVE PHILIPPS | JULY 26, 2017

COLORADO SPRINGS — Joining the Navy was one of the best decisions Alec Kerry said she had ever made. The other was coming out as transgender.

"The Navy taught me how people can come together and work hard to achieve something bigger than themselves," said Petty Officer Kerry, 24, who is training to operate nuclear reactors and soon plans to adopt the name Eva. "Strangely enough, I think what the Navy taught us about integrity was what gave me the courage to come out. I had to be honest about who I was with myself and the people I served with."

Like thousands of other transgender veterans and members of the military, she grappled with a mix of anger, sadness and fear on

Staff Sgt. Ashlee Bruce said her Air Force commanders and peers were fully supportive when she announced her gender transition.

Wednesday after President Trump tweeted that the United States military would no longer "accept or allow" transgender people to serve — a surprise move that came a year after the Obama administration permitted transgender troops to serve openly.

Some transgender troops were left to wonder if they would face a quick discharge from the military or if scheduled medical appointments would be canceled. And nearly all expressed dismay at what they saw as a misguided action that could purge the military of untold numbers of highly skilled and dedicated service members, bringing back an era when many troops lived in secrecy and shame.

Petty Officer Kerry, who has been taking estrogen for months, said starting to become a woman lifted a cloud that allowed her to perform better at work, but now she is likely to have to stop treatment.

"People are fearful," said Laila Ireland, who was an Army combat medic for 13 years before transitioning to a woman and becoming the membership director for Sparta, an L.G.B.T. military group with more than 500 active-duty members. "All morning I've been telling them, Continue to exceed the expectations, show what you are worth."

Her husband, Logan Ireland, an Air Force staff sergeant who is also transgender, could not be reached because he was in a combat leadership course, but said in a text message from the field, "I would love for my president to meet me," adding that he would like to tell Mr. Trump about all the "honorably serving transgender military members that are fighting right now for their liberties and for their country."

There are an estimated 2,000 to 11,000 active-duty transgender service members, according to a 2016 RAND Corporation study commissioned by the Pentagon. Since the Obama administration lifted the ban on transgender people serving, public opinion has been mixed. A poll conducted by Rasmussen Reports in June found that 23 percent of those surveyed believed that having them serve openly was good for the military, 38 percent said it would have no impact and 31 percent said it would hurt.

But enlisting transgender people and paying for their medical transition has become a political flash point, and there has been strong resistance. A monument to transgender veterans unveiled in June at Abraham Lincoln National Cemetery in Illinois was almost immediately defaced by vandals.

"I thought we were at a place of progress, and it feels like we're taking 10 steps back," said Umut Dursun, 35, a former Marine in Miami who transitioned from female to male after his service. He was sitting in a V.A. waiting room on Wednesday morning when he saw the news. "We're not afraid of bullets flying at us," he said. "But we are afraid of someone's experience around gender because we don't understand it."

Some conservatives say transgender troops require too many medical procedures that would undermine the military's fighting capability, and they hailed Wednesday's announcement.

Tony Perkins, a Marine veteran who is now president of the Family Research Council, a conservative advocacy group, issued a statement praising Mr. Trump "for keeping his promise to return to military priorities — and not continue the social experimentation of the Obama era that has crippled our nation's military."

Representative Vicky Hartzler, Republican of Missouri, recently offered an amendment that would have barred the military from paying for sex reassignment surgery. In a statement, Ms. Hartzler praised Mr. Trump for taking "decisive action."

"With the challenges we are facing across the globe, we are asking the American people to invest their hard-earned money in national defense," she said. "Each dollar needs to be spent to address threats facing our nation."

Transgender troops pushed back hard on the medical cost arguments, noting that the estimated $2.4 million to $8.4 million a year it would cost for care was a fraction of the $41 million the Department of Defense spent on Viagra in 2014.

One National Guard intelligence sergeant named Mac, who did not want to give his full name because he now fears being discharged, worried that the cost of investigations to ferret out closeted transgender troops could eclipse the costs of providing medical care, and in the process drive away career service members.

"The government has invested hundreds of thousands of dollars into my training and my skill set," he said. "That's not easy to replace."

Traditional veterans groups, including the Veterans of Foreign Wars and the American Legion, whose memberships tend to be older and more conservative, have been silent on the issue, but Iraq and Afghanistan Veterans of America, which represents the newest generation of fighters, came out strongly against the president's position.

"This is backward, harmful and contrary to American values. It's also bad for national security," said Paul Rieckhoff, the group's founder. "Thousands of transgender troops are serving in our military right now. An unknown number are in combat zones today."

Some young troops said they often did not know they were transgender before they joined, and developed a sense of service and of self that now feel inseparably bound.

"At lot of us grew up not really feeling we belonged," said Staff Sgt. Ashlee Bruce of the Air Force, who dresses as female at home but at work uses her birth name, Matthew. "The military took us and made us part of a team. They said, Hey, you are important to us."

Like many others interviewed, Sergeant Bruce said commanders and peers had shown nothing but support when she announced, after a deployment to Africa, that she was transitioning. Buckley Air Force Base in Colorado, where the sergeant works, even had her do a public service video about her experience.

Sergeant Bruce is scheduled to be evaluated for hormone therapy in a few weeks. If, instead, she is discharged, she said she would have no regrets because the military helped her realize who she wants to be.

"I love the Air Force," she said. "And I owe the Air Force a debt. I'm going to keep coming into work every day and doing the best I can until they tell me don't come to work any more."

Pentagon Approves Gender-Reassignment Surgery for Service Member

BY HELENE COOPER | NOV. 14, 2017

WASHINGTON — The Pentagon approved a gender-reassignment surgery for an active-duty military member, defense officials said on Tuesday, four months after President Trump abruptly announced a ban on transgender people serving in the military.

The surgery is the latest setback to Mr. Trump's effort to put a ban in place. Two weeks ago, a federal judge temporarily blocked the ban, ruling that the justification for it was suspect and most likely unconstitutional.

Even before the ruling, officials at the Defense Department had been slow-walking Mr. Trump's orders, telling transgender members of the military that they could continue to serve openly while the Pentagon decided how to handle the ban.

In announcing the ban in July, Mr. Trump posted on Twitter that United States forces could not afford the "tremendous medical costs and disruption" of transgender service members. He said he had consulted with generals and military experts, but Jim Mattis, the defense secretary, was given only a day's notice of the decision.

The RAND Corporation, in a 2016 study, found that allowing transgender people to serve openly in the military would "have minimal impact on readiness and health care costs" for the Pentagon. It estimated that health care costs would rise $2.4 million to $8.4 million a year, representing an increase of 0.04 to 0.13 percent in spending. Citing research into other countries that allow transgender people to serve, the study projected "little or no impact on unit cohesion, operational effectiveness or readiness" in the United States.

The sex-reassignment surgery is the clearest sign yet that Mr. Trump's ban is a long way from being put into effect. Dana W. White, the chief Pentagon spokeswoman, said in a statement that the individual who underwent the surgery had already started a sex-reassignment course of treatment and that the individual's doctor said the surgery was medically necessary.

"Military hospitals do not have the surgical expertise to perform this type of surgery, therefore it was conducted in a private hospital," Ms. White said in the statement.

The Defense Health Agency, a division of the Pentagon, granted a waiver allowing the department to cover the cost of the surgery.

The Pentagon's health insurance program "will cover this surgery in accordance with the department's interim guidance for transgender service members," Ms. White said.

A Defense Department official said that the service member who underwent the surgery, earlier reported by NBC News, identifies as a woman. She fought in Afghanistan. Two organizations representing transgender service members have taken the Trump administration to court over the ban.

Transgender People Will Be
Allowed to Enlist in the Military
as a Court Case Advances

BY HELENE COOPER | DEC. 11, 2017

WASHINGTON — Transgender people will be allowed to enlist in the military beginning Jan. 1, Defense Department officials said on Monday, a move that pauses President Trump's effort to bar transgender troops.

A federal judge allowed an October order pausing the ban to remain in effect, pending further legal review. The judge, Colleen Kollar-Kotelly of the Federal District Court in Washington, said in a ruling on Monday that the ban most likely violates constitutional rights to due process and equal protection.

She rejected the Trump administration's argument that it needs more time to prepare to process new transgender recruits for military service.

"The court is not persuaded that defendants will be irreparably injured by allowing the accession of transgender individuals into the military beginning on Jan. 1, 2018," she wrote.

Sarah Huckabee Sanders, the White House press secretary, suggested that Mr. Trump would continue to seek ways to carry out his ban. "The Department of Justice is currently reviewing the legal options to ensure the president's directive is implemented," she told reporters.

A Defense Department official said its move was partly a result of a barrage of lawsuits filed after Mr. Trump announced that he was barring transgender people from serving in the military. Later on Monday, and separately, a federal judge in Seattle also ordered a halt to the ban on transgender people serving in the military.

Mr. Trump announced the ban in a series of tweets in July. He said then that he had decided to do so after consulting with generals and military experts, although Defense Secretary Jim Mattis was given only a day's notice.

Advocates for allowing transgender people in the military said they were not yet ready to declare victory.

"What the ruling signals is that both the Pentagon and the courts have recognized that Trump was stepping out of his lane when he tweeted," said Aaron Belkin, the director of the Palm Center, which advocates on behalf of the transgender community in the military.

But, he added: "This could be a long process. We just don't know what happens next."

Since Mr. Trump gave the order, the Pentagon has slow-walked it, telling transgender members of the military that they could continue to serve openly while the Pentagon decided how to handle the ban. Last month, the Pentagon paid for gender-reassignment surgery for an active-duty military member.

Staff Sgt. Ashlee Bruce of the Air Force, who began her transition this year, said young transgender troops like her have been on edge in recent months, but noted that even after Mr. Trump announced all transgender troops would be discharged, her commanders and the medical team overseeing her transition continued to reassure her. They cleared the way for her to begin hormone treatments and have her name changed before she leaves for an assignment in South Korea in March.

"Everyone in the leadership kept saying it would be O.K.; they never wavered," she said. Though she still has to wear a man's uniform at work, she appeared in a dress for the first time at her squadron's holiday party last week, with the support of her command.

"It was the first time I could show who I really was, and everyone was so great about it," she said.

In announcing his ban, Mr. Trump tweeted that American forces could not afford the "tremendous medical costs and disruption" of transgender service members. But the RAND Corporation, in a 2016 study, found that allowing transgender people to serve openly in the military would "have minimal impact on readiness and health care costs" for the Pentagon.

It estimated that health care costs would rise $2.4 million, to $8.4 million annually, representing an infinitesimal 0.04 to 0.13 percent increase in spending. Citing research into other countries that allow transgender people to serve, the study projected "little or no impact on unit cohesion, operational effectiveness or readiness" in the United States.

In temporarily blocking the ban in October, Judge Kollar-Kotelly said that the administration's justification for it was suspect and probably unconstitutional.

Defense Department officials said that new guidelines, a reinstatement of President Barack Obama's opening of the military to transgender recruits, first reported by The Associated Press, mean that new recruits will have to undergo medical tests before enlisting.

The Obama administration announced last year that the Pentagon would start accepting transgender recruits in the summer 2017, but after taking over the department, Mr. Mattis delayed the policy's implementation until the beginning of 2018, pending further review.

Last week, the Justice Department asked a federal court to further delay implementation until the court cases involving the ban are resolved.

Carl Tobias, a professor at the University of Richmond School of Law, said the way forward "seems very uncertain."

"Many in the military seem open to the prospect of going forward, but Trump seems very opposed," he wrote in an email. "It is also possible that the government could allow people to enlist but impose such onerous conditions that few would enlist."

Critics See Echoes of 'Don't Ask, Don't Tell' in Military Transgender Ban

BY HELENE COOPER | MARCH 28, 2018

WASHINGTON — The Trump administration's latest effort at banning transgender individuals from serving in the military amounts to what legal experts said is essentially a reprise of an all-too-familiar directive at the Pentagon: the 1994 "don't ask, don't tell" policy.

A slew of medical and legal professionals have already lined up against the newest White House order, issued late Friday night, which experts said may survive only if it is backed by the Supreme Court.

That order is based on recommendations outlined by Defense Secretary Jim Mattis in a Feb. 22 memo on the circumstances under which transgender people would be allowed to join or remain in the military.

The memo by Mr. Mattis disqualified all people "who require or have undergone gender transition."

But he also recommended that, going forward, "transgender persons without a history or diagnosis of gender dysphoria, who are otherwise qualified for service, may serve, like all service members, in their biological sex." Gender dysphoria is the psychological condition of a person's discomfort with their biological gender.

The memo said that transgender troops who would be grandfathered into the system — under an Obama administration policy that allowed them to serve — could be discharged from the military if they continue to challenge the recommendations in courts.

Supporters of transgender rights said the recommendations echoed "don't ask, don't tell," which was repealed in 2010 after 17 years of requiring gay men, lesbians and bisexuals in the military to keep their sexuality a secret.

"What they've basically done is said that if you have gender dysphoria, you're out, with the exception of being grandfathered in, but if that's used against them in court, you're definitely out," said Brad

Protesters outside the White House in July 2017 after President Trump abruptly announced a ban on transgender people serving in the military.

Carson, the former Defense Department acting under secretary for personnel and readiness during the Obama administration.

"They're also basically saying that if you just keep quiet, we'll leave you alone," Mr. Carson said. He suggested that inherent contradiction is where a legal defense of the new policy could fall apart in court.

Aaron Belkin, the director of the Palm Center, which focuses on sexuality and the military, said he expects to see more lawsuits filed, including those that will seek to use contradictions within Mr. Mattis's memo as a basis for complaint.

In a report accompanying the new directive on Friday, the Pentagon said that 8,980 service members who identified as transgender were currently serving, and that 937 of those people had been given a diagnosis of gender dysphoria.

Mr. Mattis has since refused to discuss the issue, leaving transgender service members in a state of uncertainty. On Tuesday, he declined to answer questions about the new policy because it is a matter of litigation.

"This is what we do in America," Mr. Mattis told reporters at the Pentagon. "Anything I say could jeopardize the purity" of the legal case, he said.

Already, President Trump's efforts to ban transgender people from serving in the military, underway since last summer, have been blocked in court.

There are at the moment at least four court cases challenging Mr. Trump's original ban, announced in a series of Twitter posts last July. Federal judges have ordered that transgender people continue to be allowed to serve pending the resolution of lawsuits filed against the ban. Transgender recruits have continued to join the military, as well.

In November, the Pentagon approved a gender-reassignment surgery for an active-duty member of the military. That surgery came three months after Mr. Trump tweeted that "the United States Government will not accept or allow Transgender individuals to serve in any capacity in the U.S. Military."

The president said he decided to issue the ban after consulting with generals and military experts, although Mr. Mattis was given only a day's notice. Since then, the Defense Department has been scrambling to come up with an explicit policy that adheres to Mr. Trump's tweet.

In his memo, Mr. Mattis cited "substantial risks" about military personnel who seek to change or who question their gender identity.

He said that allowing some of them to serve would amount to an exemption of certain mental, physical and sex-based standards, and "could undermine readiness, disrupt unit cohesion, and impose an unreasonable burden on the military that is not conducive to military effectiveness and lethality."

Mr. Mattis's assertion contradicts a 2016 study by the RAND Corporation, which found that allowing transgender people to serve in the military would "have minimal impact on readiness and health care costs" for the Pentagon.

The study estimated that health care costs would rise $2.4 million to $8.4 million a year, representing an infinitesimal 0.04 to 0.13 percent increase in spending. It concluded that there were 2,000 to 11,000 active-duty troops who are transgender.

Citing research into other countries that allow transgender people to serve, the study projected "little or no impact on unit cohesion, operational effectiveness or readiness" in the United States.

In his recommendation to Mr. Trump, Mr. Mattis said the RAND study "heavily caveated data to support its conclusions, glossed over the impacts of health care costs, readiness, and unit cohesion, and erroneously relied on the selective experiences of foreign militaries with different operational requirements than our own."

"In short," Mr. Mattis concluded, "this policy issue has proven more complex than the prior administration or RAND assumed."

On Wednesday, two former surgeons general described themselves as "troubled" by Mr. Mattis's recommendations.

"The Defense Department's report on transgender military service has mischaracterized the robust body of peer-reviewed research on the effectiveness of transgender medical care as demonstrating 'considerable scientific uncertainty,' " Dr. M. Joycelyn Elders and Dr. David Satcher wrote in a joint statement.

CHAPTER 4

The Future of the Military and U.S. Veterans

Like the rest of the United States, the military is facing a changing present and an uncertain future. What will war look like in the age of cyberattacks? Will the government find working strategies to support new military ventures? Will veterans receive improved plans for retirement, health care and reparations for the sacrifices they have made for the United States? As the military and the country look to the future, there are many questions regarding the conditions of U.S. military service, defense and development.

Forces Align Against a New Military Branch to 'Win Wars' in Space

BY EMILY COCHRANE | JULY 26, 2017

WASHINGTON — As legislators look toward consolidating the hefty annual defense spending bill recently passed in the House with its Senate equivalent, one of the most unexpected debates is over a proposal to create a Space Corps, which already is facing high-level opposition from the Pentagon.

The House approved a plan that would create a Space Corps within the Air Force to oversee military operations in that emerging, and important, domain of military competition, and it would be organized similarly to how the Marine Corps is a distinct service under the Navy.

The Air Force Academy near Colorado Springs. If a military spending bill is approved, the Air Force will be required to establish a separate Space Corps by 2019.

The Space Corps would be the first newly created military branch since the Air Force in 1947.

The House vision for the Space Corps is included in the National Defense Authorization Act, the annual set of policy directions given to the military through financial guidelines. If the legislation is approved, the Air Force will be required to establish the separate branch — an entity that would defend American interests in space, organize and train its own forces and ensure commanders can "fight and win wars" in space — before Jan. 1, 2019.

Even as committees continue to tweak the bill, the proposal faces opposition from a formidable array of skeptics, including Defense Secretary Jim Mattis, members of the Joint Chiefs of Staff, Air Force leadership and even the White House.

"The Pentagon is complicated enough," said the secretary of the Air Force, Heather Wilson, while testifying before the Senate Armed

Services Committee on June 22. "We are trying to simplify it. This will make it more complex, to add more boxes to the organizational chart, and it costs more money. And if I had more money I would put it into lethality and not bureaucracy."

The White House called the proposal "premature" while Mr. Mattis, when asked about the Space Corps on July 14, laughed and said, "We'll see."

Representative Jim Cooper, Democrat of Tennessee and the ranking member of the Subcommittee on Strategic Forces, said the Air Force needed an immediate congressional push to match what he, the subcommittee chairman, Representative Mike D. Rogers, Republican of Alabama, and other legislators see as potentially threatening progress from China and Russia.

"Their record of embracing new technology is not the best," Mr. Cooper said of the Air Force, adding that the proposal would allow the Air Force staff to devise the Space Corps. "I'm hopeful they will see the light and embrace this new approach."

Col. Patrick Ryder, an Air Force spokesman, declined to comment directly on pending legislation or individual critiques of military policy.

"I think our record speaks for itself in terms of being a leader in space," he said. "One thing we can all agree on is that space superiority for our nation is critical, so we appreciate the attention the issue is getting right now."

An amendment that would have stopped the Space Corps's creation in favor of studying different solutions to the challenge was not granted a hearing on the House floor.

"Congress just hasn't done its work yet," said Representative Michael R. Turner, Republican of Ohio, who proposed the amendment. "It should be fully debated and considered before that significant step is taken."

Mr. Cooper said the threats articulated in classified briefings with intelligence officials warranted more immediate action, citing "eroding dominance" in satellite and related technology.

"Study is a congressional word for kill," he said. "We have got to act."

The bill, which passed 344 to 81 with bipartisan support from 227 Republicans and 117 Democrats, also authorized up to $696 billion in spending for the Department of Defense for the new fiscal year.

"Sounds like a solution in search of a problem," said Senator Tom Cotton, Republican of Arkansas, and chairman of the Senate Armed Services subcommittee on air and land power.

Senate agreement will most likely depend on how successful the Air Force can be in lobbying against the idea and on the decision of Senator John McCain, Republican of Arizona, the chairman of the Armed Services Committee, whose office revealed last Wednesday that he has brain cancer. "Senator McCain rules the committee with an iron hand, so a lot of it will be his decision," Mr. Cotton said, speaking before news broke about Mr. McCain's diagnosis.

The Senate has yet to formally vote on its version of the military bill, which has cleared the Armed Services Committee but has been overshadowed by the defeat of the health care legislation at the forefront of leadership priorities. It is unclear when the bill will reach the floor for debate.

"I'm skeptical," Brian Weeden, director of program planning for Secure World Foundation, an organization that studies the international use of space, said of the Space Corps's chances of success. "The Senate doesn't seem to be a fan."

The bureaucratic conundrum over how to manage space stems from a congressional commission led by Donald H. Rumsfeld before his appointment as defense secretary in the George W. Bush administration. In its final report, the commission warned that the United States was "an attractive candidate for a space Pearl Harbor." Mr. Rumsfeld, during his tenure as defense secretary, continued to push for an overhaul of the Pentagon's space initiatives, which are spread out across multiple branches.

Possible solutions debated in the space community, Mr. Weeden said, include an expansion into a separate branch equivalent to the Air

Force or the creation of a Space Guard, which would offer safety and law enforcement support similar to that of the Coast Guard.

"There are elements of global space war already happening," Mr. Weeden said, citing a Russian and Chinese presence in space and even signal jammers from North Korea. "What hasn't happened is the kinetic part: blowing up satellites."

Beyond the clashing solutions for the reorganization of military space management, the legislation would also authorize $72 billion more than the limitations set by the 2011 Budget Control Act. While lawmakers have circumvented the restrictions in the past, there has yet to be a legislative solution offered for this year's budget. It is a precarious situation, said Representative Adam Smith, the ranking House Armed Services Committee member, to be "in a world where we have promised more than we can possibly deliver."

"We're all living in an asteroid movie," said Mr. Smith, Democrat of Washington. "We're just not aware of it. Come Oct. 1, the asteroid is going to hit and we're going to be a massive train wreck."

Army, Struggling to Get Technology in Soldiers' Hands, Tries the Unconventional

BY HELENE COOPER | MARCH 18, 2018

WASHINGTON — The platoon of Army Special Operations soldiers was on a routine night patrol in eastern Afghanistan when one of them suddenly opened fire on what looked to the others to be a bush.

The bush, it turned out, had been obscuring a militant fighter. He was detectable only to the one platoon member wearing prototype night vision goggles that could detect heat signatures — a happenstance that Army officials say probably saved many lives.

That incident took place in 2015. Three years later, soldiers in the field still do not have the new night vision goggles, and that is just one example of a process that can take a decade to get new weapons from the lab to the hands of troops. Worried about that lag, the Army is creating a new and decidedly unconventional department to address it: the Futures Command.

"Washington and Marshall are looking over me like ghosts," said Ryan McCarthy, a former Ranger who is now the Army under secretary, in a reference to George Washington and George Marshall, two of the most famous proponents of an American Army that keeps ahead of all adversaries. "Things can take too long; historically services will experiment things to death and never buy anything, or don't experiment and then buy a billion-dollar PowerPoint. We have to move away from that."

So on March 26, top Army leaders will travel to Huntsville, Ala., to announce details of their plan for the Futures Command, which will focus solely on developing new weapons and getting them "downrange" faster. The doors of the command are expected to open by the end of July, and it is supposed to be fully operational a year after that.

The Futures Command, Army leaders say, is part of a movement to get the Army, focused for nearly two decades on fighting Islamist militants in Afghanistan and Iraq, in shape to fight a potential great-power land war.

At the Pentagon, the talk inside the military's biggest service is all about "modernization" and "readiness," the favorite children of the Army chief of staff, Gen. Mark A. Milley. Besides speeding up the lengthy procurement process, Army leaders want to get rid of layers of bureaucracy that can eat away at the military's competitive edge.

And they want to enlist the talents of Americans who may not necessarily see themselves as bound for the military, by locating the Futures Command not at a traditional military base like Fort Hood, Tex., or Fort Sill, Okla., but in a city with easy access to big universities and cutting-edge technological research.

Seattle, San Francisco and Boston are all among the cities Army planners say they are looking at for the Futures Command. Mark T. Esper, the secretary of the Army, said that whoever is chosen to lead the command will be "not a traditional person who spent all their time in combat units, but someone who understands the acquisition process, and who understands the corporate Army." Ten cities should be selected within the next two months as finalists for hosting the command.

The Army is making many of the changes in an effort to figure out how to fight multiple types of wars at the same time.

More than 16 years of counterinsurgency warfare has taught military leaders one thing: The burden of fighting jihadists in multiple places is unlikely to go away anytime soon. Even today, almost eight years after President Barack Obama announced the end of combat in Iraq and three years after he announced the end of combat in Afghanistan, American troops are deployed in both countries, not to mention Syria, Niger, Somalia, Libya and Mali.

But at the same time, the Army has been charged with getting ready for a possible war on the Korean Peninsula. President Trump

Soldiers practicing with a howitzer artillery piece last month at Fort Sill. The Futures Command wants to make howitzers more effective from afar, keeping soldiers out of enemies' target range.

may have agreed to one-on-one talks with North Korea's leader, Kim Jong-un, but the Pentagon is still trying to make sure that American forces are ready for what would probably be a completely different kind of war.

General Milley, the Army chief of staff, has repeatedly expressed concern that the Army has lost what he calls its "muscle memory" of how to fight big land wars. Beyond that, Army leaders — many of them students of history — say that for almost 200 years, the Army has often gotten the first battle of major wars wrong.

In particular, General Milley has cited the ill-fated Battle of Kasserine Pass during World War II, when unprepared American troops were outfoxed and pummeled by German forces. And he has mentioned Task Force Smith, the small, poorly equipped unit mauled by North Korean troops in 1950 during the Korean War.

The quickest way to guard against a repeat of these debacles, Army planners say, is to emphasize readiness and to streamline the process for getting new technology to soldiers.

At Fort Sill, where 16 percent of Army recruits go through basic training and soldiers learn long-range artillery maneuvers, Futures Command leaders will consult directly with troops about how to update artillery pieces to improve speed and range.

On a cold afternoon on the artillery field last month, soldiers were training to fire the Paladin, a decades-old tracked vehicle that moves along with Army units and can fire at a distance. A few hundred yards away, a handful of soldiers were using another piece, the howitzer, for artillery practice.

These are the pieces Futures Command will seek to update, Army leaders said, with an aim of making them more effective from a distance — putting American soldiers out of the target range of adversaries.

The same concept is at work with new night vision goggle cameras that can be mounted on weapons and feed an image to the goggles. In essence, explained Sgt. Eric Janson, an Army weapons squad leader, "whatever your rifle is pointed at, you can see in a heads-up display" in your goggles. That means a soldier could, for instance, position a rifle above his head, squat and take cover, and still shoot a target.

The goggles cost $23,000 each. Army leaders say they hope to reduce the price over time, as they buy in bulk. But it will not come down much; the old ones were still $15,000 each. They say they hope to have them in soldiers' hands, finally, sometime this year.

Pentagon Puts Cyberwarriors on the Offensive, Increasing the Risk of Conflict

BY DAVID E. SANGER | JUNE 17, 2018

WASHINGTON — The Pentagon has quietly empowered the United States Cyber Command to take a far more aggressive approach to defending the nation against cyberattacks, a shift in strategy that could increase the risk of conflict with the foreign states that sponsor malicious hacking groups.

Until now, the Cyber Command has assumed a largely defensive posture, trying to counter attackers as they enter American networks. In the relatively few instances when it has gone on the offensive, particularly in trying to disrupt the online activities of the Islamic State and its recruiters in the past several years, the results have been mixed at best.

But in the spring, as the Pentagon elevated the command's status, it opened the door to nearly daily raids on foreign networks, seeking to disable cyberweapons before they can be unleashed, according to strategy documents and military and intelligence officials.

The change in approach was not formally debated inside the White House before it was issued, according to current and former administration officials. But it reflects the greater authority given to military commanders by President Trump, as well as a widespread view that the United States has mounted an inadequate defense against the rising number of attacks aimed at America.

It is unclear how carefully the administration has weighed the various risks involved if the plan is acted on in classified operations. Adversaries like Russia, China and North Korea, all nuclear-armed states, have been behind major cyberattacks, and the United States has struggled with the question of how to avoid an unforeseen escalation as it wields its growing cyberarsenal.

Another complicating factor is that taking action against an adversary often requires surreptitiously operating in the networks of an ally, like Germany — a problem that often gave the Obama administration pause.

The new strategy envisions constant, disruptive "short of war" activities in foreign computer networks. It is born, officials said, of more than a decade of counterterrorism operations, where the United States learned that the best way to take on Al Qaeda or the Islamic State was by destroying the militants inside their bases or their living rooms. The objective, according to the new "vision statement" quietly issued by the command, is to "contest dangerous adversary activity before it impairs our national power."

Pushing American defenses "as close as possible to the origin of adversary activity extends our reach to expose adversaries' weaknesses, learn their intentions and capabilities, and counter attacks close to their origins," the document says. "Continuous engagement imposes tactical friction and strategic costs on our adversaries, compelling them to shift resources to defense and reduce attacks."

Another Pentagon document, dated May 2017, provides a legal basis for attacking nuclear missiles on the launchpad using "nonkinetic options" — meaning a cyberattack or some other means that does not involve bombing a missile on the pad or otherwise blowing it up.

The policy was issued two months after The New York Times revealed that the Obama administration had developed an extensive "left of launch" capability to attack North Korea's missiles using cyber and electronic warfare, though it was unclear how well the strategy was working. The new Pentagon legal strategy was first reported by The Daily Beast.

As the Defense Department elevated the Cyber Command to a status equal to the Indo-Pacific Command, the European Command, the Space Command and the Joint Special Operations Command, among others, it declared that most of its 133 "cyber mission teams" were combat-ready after years of development.

But most of those teams protect Defense Department networks.

Offensive cyberaction by the United States has been relatively rare, a reflection of the time it takes to mount operations and the fact that only the president can approve any use of a cyberweapon that is likely to have significant effects. Those operations have included disabling another nation's nuclear facilities or its missiles, as the United States has attempted in Iran and North Korea, or disrupting the communications of groups like the Islamic State.

The president's sole authority to authorize the use of those weapons is similar to his authority to launch nuclear weapons, a recognition that cyberweapons, even if less powerful than nuclear arms, can have broad, unintended effects.

Under the Trump administration, the traditional structure of White House oversight of American offensive and defensive cyberactivities is being dismantled. Days after taking office in April, the new national security adviser, John R. Bolton, forced out the homeland security adviser, Thomas P. Bossert, in part because of his discomfort that Mr. Bossert had direct access to the president.

Mr. Bolton then eliminated the position of White House cybercoordinator, who had overseen the complex mix of cyberactivities run by the American government. The last person who held the job, Rob Joyce, had previously run the Tailored Access Operations unit of the National Security Agency — the covert "special forces" of America's cyberoperations, which has mounted attacks on critical foreign targets, from Iran's nuclear facilities to North Korean missile testing sites. Mr. Joyce returned to the N.S.A.

American intelligence agencies have identified cyberthreats as the No. 1 risk facing the United States — it has ranked ahead of terrorism for years now in the annual assessment provided to Congress, even before the Russian intrusion into the election. But the White House declared that it did not need a separate cybercoordinator because the issues are included in many other programs. A young National Security Council staff member, with scant experience in the topic, now oversees offensive cyberissues.

The United States Cyber Command was created partly in response to a Russian hacking attack that long predated the 2016 election. In the fall of 2008, Russian intelligence agencies penetrated SIPRNet, the Pentagon's secret internal network; that led to a rush to consolidate several cyberprograms into a command. The Chinese, meanwhile, were stealing weapons designs, including blueprints for the F-35, America's most expensive fighter jet.

Cyber Command was placed at Fort Meade, Md., home of the National Security Agency, but it has been criticized for being far too dependent on the N.S.A.'s hacking skills.

A decade later, it is under new command, led by Gen. Paul Nakasone. He was a junior officer in the command's early days and was deeply involved in one of its first big classified projects, "Nitro Zeus": the plan to use cybertools, among other things, to take down Iran's air defenses, its communications systems and its power grid if a conflict broke out.

To prepare for that day, if it ever happened, the United States tunneled deep inside Iran's grids, and even Revolutionary Guards Corps command-and-control systems. It was a huge mission, involving hundreds of troops and civilians.

The program was never activated; the 2015 Iran nuclear agreement avoided conflict. But now that Mr. Trump has announced that he is abandoning the accord, many of those plans are being dusted off, according to several officials.

General Nakasone, in his confirmation hearings in March, made clear that a more aggressive approach to opponents in cyberspace would be needed, though he gave few details. "By conducting operations to frustrate and counter adversary cyberactivities to decrease will, increase cost and deny benefits," he said, the United States could begin to deliver more decisive blows with its attacks.

The same month, Gen. John E. Hyten, the head of Strategic Command, said in testimony that if the United States was going to defend itself in cyberspace, it needed clear rules of day-to-day engagement.

"Cyberspace needs to be looked at as a warfighting domain," he said, "and if somebody threatens us in cyberspace, we need to have the authorities to respond." His statement seemed to reflect a view that the current legal authority is too slow.

There is little debate inside the government's sprawling community of cyberwarriors and defenders that the United States needs to step up its game: It did not see the Russian hack of the 2016 election coming, or North Korea's "WannaCry" attack last year, which crippled the National Health Service in Britain and rippled around the world, partly driven by stolen American cyberweapons.

But the risks of escalation — of United States action in foreign networks leading to retaliatory strikes against American banks, dams, financial markets or communications networks — are considerable, according to current and former officials. Mr. Trump has shown only a cursory interest in the subject, former aides say, not surprising for a man who does not use a computer and came of age as a business executive in a predigital era.

Efforts to rewrite the main document governing the presidential authorities in the cyberarena — Presidential Policy Directive 20, signed by Barack Obama — have faltered in the chaos of Mr. Bolton's decision to oust the key players.

"It is essentially a 'forward defense' approach," Jason Healey, who runs the cyber initiative at Columbia University, said recently. "Clearly, what we have been doing so far isn't working. But you want to think through the consequences carefully."

The chief risk is that the internet becomes a battleground of all-against-all, as nations not only place "implants" in the networks of their adversaries — something the United States, China, Russia, Iran and North Korea have done with varying levels of sophistication — but also begin to engage in daily attack and counterattack.

Military Is Overhauling
Its Retirement Systems

BY ANN CARRNS | NOV. 3, 2017

ABOUT 1.7 MILLION PEOPLE serving in the United States armed forces have a big decision to make in the coming months, as the military undertakes a major overhaul of its retirement system.

Beginning in January, the military is switching from just a traditional pension system, in which retirees receive a monthly check for life based on their pay and years of service, to one that also includes investment accounts, like those commonly available to civilian workers. The new "blended" system is based, in part, on recommendations by the Military Compensation and Retirement Modernization Commission.

The system needed updating, the commission said, because the military's current pension system leaves a vast majority of service members with no retirement savings when they leave the military. Currently, service members must serve at least 20 years to get a pension — hence its "20 or nothing" nickname. More than 80 percent of service members leave the military short of that minimum, according to the Defense Department.

The new system still offers a monthly pension, but one calculated with a formula that reduces it by 20 percent, said Michael Meese, a retired Army brigadier general and chief operating officer of the American Armed Forces Mutual Aid Association, a nonprofit group that provides insurance and other financial services to military members. (The commission's final report noted that while its benefits recommendations weren't "budget driven," they would nevertheless "substantially reduce" government spending.)

But service members will also receive contributions to the Thrift Savings Plan, the federal government's version of an investment-based 401(k) retirement plan. The military will contribute a minimum of

1 percent of the service member's pay, even if he or she contributes nothing. The military will also chip in as much as 4 percent more in matching contributions, for a maximum government contribution of 5 percent.

(Service members already may contribute to the Thrift Savings Plan, known for its low-cost investment funds, but the military currently makes no contributions.)

"It's no longer all or nothing," said Josh Andrews, an Air Force reservist and a certified financial planner with USAA, a financial services company focused mainly on service members and their families.

Service members will also be eligible for midcareer bonuses aimed at encouraging them to extend their time in the military.

Another new and somewhat controversial component gives those who reach the 20-year retirement minimum the option of taking part of their pension as a lump sum in exchange for a reduced benefit. This option must be considered carefully, Mr. Andrews said, because while it could be helpful to meet an immediate financial need — like starting a business or paying off a large debt — it provides "less money in your pocket over time" than a pension taken in the usual way.

Men and women enlisting in the armed forces after Dec. 31 will be automatically enrolled in the blended system. (They'll start getting the 1 percent contribution to the Thrift Savings Plan in 60 days, but must wait two years for matching contributions.) People with 12 or more years of service at the end of this year will be "grandfathered" into the current system.

Service members with less than 12 years of service, however, must decide whether to move to the new system or remain in the old one. In general, the decision to switch to the blended system is "irrevocable," according to the Defense Department.

Both Mr. Andrews and Mr. Meese suggested that people who knew for sure that they did not want to stay in the military for 20 years would probably benefit from switching to the blended system. Those who are committed to remaining, however, may want to stay with the current plan — although there are still risks. The military, like private employers, can go through periods of downsizing, Mr. Andrews noted, in which case staying in the old system could leave you short.

It matters where someone is in his or her career, Mr. Andrews said. "If someone is at the 10-year point," he said, "it's much less risky to stay in the old system than if you're one to two years in."

Those who are unsure of their plans, Mr. Meese said, have some hard thinking to do. Are you likely to save 5 percent on your own, to get the full matching contribution in the Thrift Savings Plan? If not, you may be better off in the old system. Merely getting the 1 percent automatic contribution is unlikely to make up for the 20 percent reduction in your pension if you do stay until retirement, he said.

To help weigh the options, the Defense Department is requiring all service members to take a two-hour online training course. "We want to make sure they make an informed decision," said Henry Manning, operations officer for the assistant secretary of the Army for manpower and reserve affairs.

Buoyed by Financial Support, Military Veterans Are a Growing Part of the Paralympics

BY BEN SHPIGEL | MARCH 18, 2018

PYEONGCHANG, SOUTH KOREA — Rusty Schieber, the United States wheelchair curling coach, has a theory about the future of the American Paralympic movement. It echoes the past.

The Stoke Mandeville Games, the forerunner of the Paralympics, were established in 1948 to restore a sense of purpose to veterans and civilians injured during World War II. As exposure and opportunities increased, American veterans developed a deep connection to the Paralympics, assuming progressively prominent roles on Team U.S.A.

They accounted for 24.3 percent (18 of 74) of the American roster here at the 2018 event, which ended Sunday with the United States atop the medal table with 36. Veterans were 22.5 percent (18 of 80) of the team four years ago in Sochi, Russia, and 10 percent (5 of 50) eight years ago in Vancouver, British Columbia. As Schieber sees it, those figures will only swell in the coming years, even as worldwide conflicts have declined, because of one reason.

"It's moving toward an organization disproportionately composed of military veterans because of the funding that veterans are eligible for and civilians are not," Schieber said.

In many cases, pursuing Paralympic glory places a financial strain on American athletes, who receive sport-specific stipends from the United States Olympic Committee but also seek out grants and hold fund-raisers to offset costs associated with travel and equipment. All that also applies to veterans. But at every stage of the process, from their introduction to a sport to competing in it on an international level, they are eligible for assistance that further subsidizes their quest.

Two of the five members of the United States wheelchair curling team at the Paralympics are military veterans.

"Thankfully we're not getting as many kids blown up as we used to, but there are more avenues for the veterans to get some of those financial burdens lifted," said Nico Marcolongo, the senior manager of Operation Rebound, a program for veterans and emergency medical workers affiliated with the Challenged Athletes Foundation. He added, "If all things are equal, it's harder for a nonveteran to get their start and get their resources than it would be for a veteran."

Schieber, who served in the Air Force from 1985 to 1992, has no patience for those who criticize the imbalance, but he is aware of it. The uneven playing field has ramifications on recruiting, roster composition and team dynamics; Schieber suggested that in the past he needed to quell resentment over the discrepancy. None of the five curlers on the 2018 team, two of whom served in the Army, indicated in interviews that there was anything close to a rift.

"That athlete can train almost full time, in effect," said Schieber, acknowledging that the athlete might then improve at a faster rate than a civilian. "We're not paying him to be an athlete, but he's getting totally subsidized by a third party, the U.S. government. He can live a pretty good financial life. He doesn't have to have that second job. It's hugely unlevel, but I don't care. If you're a veteran, take every penny you can get."

The biggest help comes from the monthly allowance provided by the Department of Veterans Affairs, which is given only to athletes who are training or competing at a high level as defined by their sport's governing body. A V.A. spokesman said 16 of the 18 veterans on the United States team here received an allowance.

Based on the number of dependents in the athlete's family, that monthly stipend ranges from $617 to more than $1,100. Any veteran who receives the allowance, then, automatically makes at least $7,400 more than a civilian on the same team.

Before they are eligible to earn this extra money, veterans first must be exposed to a sport. From his experience, Schieber said, veterans who want to participate in outreach camps around the country can have their expenses covered by V.A. hospitals or private organizations. Then they must unearth sources of funding that abet their continued involvement.

Often, veterans turn to organizations like Operation Rebound, which awards an average of $1,500 in need-based grants to athletes, regardless of skill level, whose applications are accepted, and the Semper Fi Fund.

Jimmy Sides, a former Marine, was introduced to snowboarding through the Walter Reed National Military Medical Center in Maryland, which offered trips to places like Breckenridge, Colo. Calling his advantage "almost unfair," Sides said Semper Fi provided almost all of his funding to compete, paying for gear, registration costs and race fees.

"I feel bad for the guy that loses his leg in a motorcycle accident or the cancer patient that loves snowboarding and wants to do this but has to struggle and grind," Sides said.

On the curling team, Justin Marshall, who did not serve in the military but said that many members of his family did, works 40 hours a week as an architectural associate and spends about 20 hours practicing. Last year, he took about two months of unpaid leave and was responsible for costs of domestic travel.

In an interview at the Utica Curling Club in Whitesboro, N.Y., before the Paralympics, Marshall said that his situation was hard, but that he would never hold that against his teammates who were veterans.

"Almost every guy in my family served in the military, and I probably would have followed except I had my spinal cord stroke when I was 12," he said. "It helps them, so I can't be mad at them for it. I wish I had that extra funding, but I don't, so I just try to find another way to take care of that."

His teammate Steve Emt, who served in the Army, teaches seventh-grade math in Connecticut, where, to his eternal gratitude, the school board grants him time off to compete. Emt, a former walk-on basketball player at the University of Connecticut who became a paraplegic from a car accident in 1995, recruits veterans to curling.

"I was told that I could be a Paralympian," Emt said. "Being a young sport, it's a big selling point. The chances of vets making the basketball team are slim. So, come curl. If we can tell them, 'Hey, we've got a trip to the U.S. Open in New York that could be fully funded for you because you're a veteran, come on up and play and learn the sport,' they'll be hooked."

Rick Adams, the United States Olympic Committee's chief of Paralympics, agreed that infrastructure and support for veterans across the nascent stages of an athlete's development were beneficial, but he hesitated to say that could be parlayed into an increased presence on the American team.

"It's a possibility, but most of the time what you find is that they may not have been in a sport for a long time," Adams said. "I think there's a balance between someone who's been participating for a long period of time and someone who's been in the military for a long time and then they're in a situation where they're Paralympic-eligible and take up a sport. I don't know I would extrapolate out to say that they're at an advantage."

The U.S.O.C. bases how much money to award sports in the Olympics and Paralympics on many factors, but above all success. It is unlikely that the wheelchair curlers, who have yet to medal since the sport was added in 2006 and finished in last place here out of 12 nations, will receive more money than in the past. And so Schieber, to improve the team's fortunes in the future, might be more likely to recruit as many military veterans as possible: He knows that they'd be more likely to afford the expenses to compete.

"If I'm looking at two athletes that are absolutely equal, does it fall into my mind that the veteran may have the better opportunity for funding and may be long-term a better athlete down the road?" Schieber said. "You hate to say it. That's a rhetorical question. I can't give you an answer."

An answer could come as soon as 2020, at the Tokyo Paralympics. The proportion of veterans has steadily increased in the Summer Paralympics, too, from 7.51 percent (16 of 213) of the United States roster in Beijing 10 years ago to 12.4 percent (33 of 267) two years ago in Rio de Janeiro.

Those numbers are not quite what they were 70 years ago at the Stoke Mandeville Games, of course. But maybe the United States Paralympic team is on its way.

Suit Calls Navy Board Biased Against Veterans With PTSD

BY DAVE PHILIPPS | MARCH 2, 2018

THINGS GOT UGLY for Cpl. Tyson Manker in Iraq. During a firefight in the confusion of the 2003 invasion, the 21-year-old Marine shot up a bus full of civilians. Later, during a chase, he dropped an Iraqi in a flowing white robe with a shot to the torso, only to discover afterward that he had hit a teenage girl. His squad beat detainees, and accidentally shot several other civilians.

After his deployment, Corporal Manker was kicked out of the Marine Corps with an other-than-honorable discharge — not for anything that happened in combat, but for smoking marijuana to try to quiet his nerves when he got home.

The military has increasingly acknowledged in recent years that there are tens of thousands of Corporal Mankers — troops whose brutal experiences left them with post-traumatic stress disorder, and who were then pushed out of the military for misconduct. Many were given other-than-honorable discharges that stripped them of veterans' benefits.

The Army and Air Force have moved in recent years to make it easier for these veterans to get their discharges upgraded to honorable. But not the Marine Corps.

The office that oversees discharges for the Navy and Marines, the Naval Discharge Review Board, rejects nearly 85 percent of requests for upgrades relating to PTSD, compared with 45 percent for the Army board.

Mr. Manker, now 36, applied for an upgrade in 2016 and was turned down. "It seems like the board doesn't even look at the issues," he said in an interview. "They just say no."

A group from the Yale Law School filed a federal class-action lawsuit on Friday against the Navy on behalf of Mr. Manker and other

Navy and Marine veterans, arguing that behind their denials was "a systemic institutional bias or secret policy that discriminates against applicants who suffer from PTSD."

The case, filed in New Haven, Conn., is the latest in a series of lawsuits by the university's Veterans Legal Services Clinic, seeking recognition that vast numbers of veterans, dating back to the Vietnam era, have been improperly discharged and denied the benefits that were meant to help them re-enter society.

A main focus has been the boards for corrections of military records in each branch of the military. These boards have the power to restore a veteran's eligibility for health care and education benefits by upgrading their discharges to honorable.

The boards were created after World War II, when Congress recognized that disciplinary decisions made quickly under wartime pressure by military commanders often contained mistakes, and that in the aftermath, veterans deserved an avenue for due process to correct them, according to Jonathan Petkun, one of the Yale students who filed the lawsuit.

"We don't see that happening now," said Mr. Petkun, a former Marine captain who served in Iraq and Afghanistan. "The board seems to just be rubber stamping things."

"As a former officer, I think commanders in the field need broad discretion," he said. "But when I was an officer, I thought, if I made a mistake, veterans would have recourse. Now I see that is rarely the case."

Yale students working with veterans groups have gradually forced the Pentagon to be more open to correcting what veterans groups largely view as unfair discharges. In 2014, in response to a lawsuit by Yale and the group Vietnam Veterans of America, Defense Secretary Chuck Hagel issued new guidelines for upgrading discharges. The guidelines instructed the review boards to give "liberal consideration" to the possibility that PTSD contributed to a veteran's other-than-honorable discharge.

Tyson Manker, a former Marine corporal, is one of the plaintiffs in a class-action suit against the Navy over its handling of applications for discharge upgrades.

The Army board quickly changed course, and its denial rate for applications involving PTSD fell from 96 percent to about 45 percent, according to Department of Defense data. The Air Force made similar changes. But the Navy board, which oversees both sailors and Marines, has scarcely budged.

Brad Carson, who oversaw the Army board as an undersecretary in the Obama administration, said the boards were overworked, and had only a few minutes to review each case. But even with more time, he said, it is far from simple to reach a fair outcome in cases where a veteran clearly committed misconduct and also has a stress-disorder diagnosis.

"How do you determine how PTSD affected an action, which might also be due just to, well, being a bad soldier?" he said in an interview. "The Navy has a strong cultural belief, going back centuries, that you do not second-guess commanders. I suspect because of that, when they have a difficult case, they fall back on tradition and defer to commanders."

A Navy spokesman said that its board's staff was too busy to comment for this article.

Mr. Manker's experience, detailed in the class-action suit, shows how the Navy board currently denies upgrades even to veterans with clear diagnoses of PTSD whose enlistments ended with a single instance of relatively minor misconduct.

He had been the top-rated junior Marine in his platoon, and the first to be promoted to corporal. During the invasion of Iraq, he became a squad leader in charge of a dozen Marines.

But the stresses of combat piled up. A few weeks after the invasion, his company in the 3rd Battalion, 7th Marine Regiment, were ambushed on a crowded highway in Baghdad. In the shootout, he and several other Marines fired more than a hundred rounds into a bus. His memory is of shattering glass and looks of terror from passengers as the bus sped away. He said he had wounded and perhaps killed an unknown number of civilians.

Fighting a war with no front line against enemies with no uniforms, he saw violence meted out in similarly senseless bursts in the months that followed. He also saw casualties on his team. After a handgun accidentally went off, he had to clean the remnants of a friend's head out of a Humvee.

"There was never a chance to grieve, no time to process any of this," Mr. Manker said of his time in Iraq. "We were just expected to be Marines and deal with it."

At the end of the deployment, the Marine Corps gave everyone in his regiment a one-page questionnaire to screen for post-traumatic stress. Mr. Manker remembered marking on his questionnaire that he had been exposed to nearly every type of trauma listed, including seeing dead civilians and Marines, killing enemy fighters and civilians, and experiencing nightmares and hypervigilance. No one ever followed up, he said.

A few days after returning to the United States, he said, he smoked marijuana to try to unwind before going on leave. He was caught and discharged from the Marine Corps.

As a civilian, he spent years working in dead-end jobs and struggling with anger, depression and substance abuse. He said he considered suicide. He went to a Veterans Affairs hospital in 2004, but was told that his other-than-honorable discharge barred him from help.

He eventually received a PTSD diagnosis from two civilian therapists. He was treated privately, gradually rebuilt his life, went to college and law school, and began practicing law in Illinois, his home state. In his spare time he studied military regulations, hoping to get his discharge upgraded.

He submitted a 65-page petition to the Board for Corrections of Naval Records in 2016, and got back a denial of just a few pages, peppered with misspellings. The letter said that PTSD had not influenced his decision to smoke marijuana, and that he had made "conscious decisions to violate the tenets of honorable and faithful service."

Mr. Manker hopes the Yale class-action suit will spur the Navy board to look again at his discharge and those of hundreds of other veterans of Iraq and Afghanistan.

"So many guys and girls are in the same situation," he said. "They feel betrayed, forgotten and they don't know what to do."

Veterans Go Back to Court Over Burn Pits. Do They Have a Chance?

BY SETH HARP | MAY 17, 2018

ON MAY 9, A FEDERAL APPEALS court heard oral arguments in a case about an explosive issue among U.S. veterans: the widespread use of burn pits in Iraq and Afghanistan, and the potential health consequences they suffered as a result.

The case, which dates back to 2008, consolidated dozens of lawsuits by hundreds of veterans and their families seeking to recover damages from the military contractor KBR Inc., but a trial court dismissed it in July 2017. It could be at a legal dead end unless the panel of judges, the Fourth Circuit Court of Appeals in Richmond, Va., overturns the dismissal.

The plaintiffs accuse KBR of negligence for exposing them to toxic emissions from open-air trash fires known as burn pits, which they say cause respiratory, neurological and other health problems. In tossing the case last year, the trial court accepted KBR's argument that the American military made the decision to use burn pits to dispose of trash on bases, and that federal courts cannot second-guess the executive branch's wartime decisions.

One plaintiff, Lauren Price, a Navy veteran from Pasco County, Fla., who developed constrictive bronchiolitis after working at a burn pit in Baghdad, said in an interview that she has already given up hope. "I've stopped paying attention," she said. After 10 years of litigation, the case is still at the procedural starting gates, and unless the plaintiffs eke out a win on appeal, it will be one of the biggest setbacks yet for tens of thousands of affected veterans who have received zero recompense despite years of advocacy by lawyers and nonprofits.

The controversy is at a point where it could become the subject of a Supreme Court decision or an act of Congress. Here's a brief introduction to an issue that has risen over time from the lowest military scuttlebutt to the highest levels of American government.

What is a burn pit?

The military bases the United States maintained for eight years in Iraq and 17 years to date in Afghanistan were hardly spartan encampments. There were air-conditioned stores, fast-food restaurants, movie theaters, internet cafes and swimming pools. Soldiers bunked in prefabricated trailers and dined in spacious chow halls serving up hot square meals three times a day. All that consumption produced garbage, lots of it, which had to somehow be disposed of. The solution? Dump it into open-air pits, drench it in jet fuel and light it on fire.

On the largest American bases, like Camp Victory in Baghdad or Camp Anaconda near Balad, a perpetual miasma lingered over the tents and trailers, reeking of burnt plastic. The effect, worsened by the extreme heat, could be nauseating. Until 2010, when the Department of Defense banned burn pits, soldiers complained of coughing up "black gunk." Thousands came home from deployment with some kind of respiratory illness, mostly mild or moderate, but including career-ending lung diseases and fatal cancers. Former Vice President Joe Biden has even speculated that his son died from burn-pit exposure; Beau Biden received a rare brain-cancer diagnosis in 2013 at the age of 44, four years after a deployment to Iraq.

In 2013, in response to rising concerns from doctors and veterans' advocates, Congress directed the V.A. to set up a registry of veterans who were exposed to burn pits. More than 142,000 have signed up so far.

So burn pits cause lung disease?

Deployments are associated with an increased risk of asthma and emphysema as well as a number of rare respiratory conditions, but there are numerous factors that could contribute to these illnesses. Iraq and Afghanistan are two of the world's most polluted countries, and there are also dust storms, oil-well fires and battlefield explosions to take into account, not to mention the copious quantities of cigarettes that soldiers smoke.

In 2004, the Department of Defense asked Dr. Robert Miller of Vanderbilt University to examine a large cohort of soldiers who came back from Iraq with unexplained shortness of breath. "Soldier after soldier going from elite athlete to someone who could not complete a two-mile run," Miller said. "This is not something you see in a normal young adult — period." While their X-rays were often normal, Miller went further and performed surgical biopsies on about 60 veterans, taking tissue samples from their lungs. A majority showed evidence of constrictive bronchiolitis, an incurable disease characterized by tiny particles lodged in the airways. "There was particulate matter in all of the biopsies," Miller said. "It's clearly inhalational." Most of the soldiers Miller treated were medically discharged and received disability benefits. But after he reported his findings, the Defense Department stopped sending him patients. "They felt we had stepped over the line by doing aggressive biopsies," he said.

On May 8, a team of medical researchers published an article in the journal Experimental Lung Research in which they reported creating an animal model of burn-pit symptoms by injecting samples of dust collected from Iraq's Camp Liberty base into the tracheas of mice. One of the authors, Dr. Anthony Szema, formerly the V.A.'s chief of allergy medicine and now with Hofstra's Zucker School of Medicine, said the carbonaceous and metallic particles that lodged in the air sacs of the mice were identical to those seen in Miller's biopsies. "If you were in a burn pit, you definitely inhaled this stuff," Szema said. "And it definitely causes lung injury."

Lauren Price returned home from Iraq feeling sick and unable to explain why. Halfway through her 2007 deployment, she came down with the "creeping crud," as she called the material in her lungs, and by 2008, "I couldn't walk. I couldn't climb stairs. The crap in my lungs kept getting worse, until it was hard to breathe."

Doesn't the V.A. compensate sick veterans?

The V.A. compensates veterans for injuries and disabilities incurred as a result of military service, including illnesses and disease. But when the onset of a chronic health condition is delayed, causation can be hard to prove.

The V.A.'s current position on burn pits is that there is not enough evidence to prove a direct connection between exposure and the many health issues veterans are reporting. A 2011 government-funded assessment of existing research said there may be long-term health effects, but the evidence was lacking and the data inconclusive. The V.A. may grant disability benefits for various pulmonary ailments, including asthma, but only if the veteran proves it resulted from military service.

"The V.A. says 'Prove it,' " said Greg Lovett, who made "Delay, Deny, Hope You Die," a documentary about veterans with burn-pit symptoms trying to get benefits. "How can you prove it? You're sick, and you're trying to take care of yourself, you've got all these medical bills, you're not getting the medicine you need, appointments are getting postponed, canceled, and the burden is on you to show this is service-related."

What does KBR have to do with it?

The engineering and construction firm KBR, which made more money off the Iraq war than any other corporation, provided a wide range of logistical services to the armed forces in Iraq and in Afghanistan, which included the day-to-day operation of 119 burn pits.

Denied benefits by the V.A., many veterans went after KBR directly, filing some 63 lawsuits, including 44 class-action suits, claiming negligence and other causes of action. In 2008, the lawsuits, spread across 43 states, were consolidated into a single proceeding, Metzgar v. KBR Inc. The multidistrict litigation involves hundreds of plaintiffs, millions of pages of documents and dozens of depositions, but after 10 years it is still far from the trial phase, stalled out over the technical jurisdictional arguments that KBR's lawyers have advanced. All the litigation to date has dealt with the preliminary question of whether KBR can even be sued.

In January 2018, the judge of a workers' compensation case in the Department of Labor decided that burn-pit exposure was to blame for a KBR contractor's pulmonary condition. It was the first instance of a federal agency accepting the premise, but it was an administrative-law decision, not binding on other agencies or the courts.

Why was the lawsuit dismissed?

In July 2017, the trial court judge, Robert W. Titus of the District of Maryland, held that it was the military's decision to dispose of solid waste in burn pits, not KBR's, and that federal courts have no power to second-guess the executive branch's wartime decisions, a precedent known as the political-question doctrine. He also held that "sovereign immunity," which generally shields the federal government from being sued, extends to private contractors supporting the military in a combat zone.

The plaintiffs appealed to the Fourth Circuit, saying that Judge Titus got it wrong.

"We needn't second-guess any military decision," Susan L. Burke, lead counsel for the veterans, told the panel of appellate judges. She said the evidence shows that most of KBR's burn pits were in fact unauthorized.

Warren W. Harris, who argued the case for KBR, ridiculed that notion. "Burn pits were being operated in plain view of thousands of soldiers across two theaters of war," he said, meaning the military must have known and approved of what KBR was doing.

Even assuming that's true, Burke said, KBR violated its contract with the military by burning hazardous waste.

There is little evidence of that, Harris responded.

Price told The Times that she personally burned hazardous waste on instructions from KBR personnel, including auto parts, batteries, mattresses, styrofoam and computers. "The KBR guy sitting in an air-conditioned office would come out and take one look in the truck and say 'Dump it right there,' " she said. "For them to deny it now is insulting."

Aside from these questions of fact, the extent to which private military contractors like KBR share the government's immunity from being sued is an unsettled area of U.S. law.

"It's incoherent," said Stephen Vladeck, a professor at the University of Texas School of Law who writes for the blog Lawfare. Military contractors can be court-martialed or indicted in the United States for their actions overseas, he said, but judges are all over the map on the question of whether they can be held liable for negligence and other civil misconduct. If the Supreme Court doesn't step in to "clean up the mess," he said, Congress should pass a law making it clear one way or the other. "And if the contractors really aren't going to be held liable," he said, "by what mechanisms are they going to be held to account?"

What happens if the veterans win?

If the case is reinstated, the plaintiff veterans will still have to litigate the complex medical question of causation. KBR denies that burn pits are harmful to human health. "Military personnel deployed to Southwest Asia were exposed to many hazardous conditions, including the harsh ambient air," a representative of KBR wrote in an emailed statement. "The government's best scientific and expert opinions have repeatedly concluded there is no link between any long-term health issues and burn-pit emissions."

If the Court of Appeals upholds the dismissal, only the Supreme Court will have the power to reinstate the case.

"I don't want to sugarcoat it," Vladeck said. "The plaintiffs face an uphill battle."

Is Congress doing anything about this?

After years of inaction, Congress has shown some inclination to intervene. In 2010, lawmakers banned the military from using burn pits except where there was no feasible alternative. In 2013, Congress mandated the creation of the V.A. registry, and the 2018 defense-spending bill required the V.A. to coordinate further research on the effects of burn pits. On May 1, members of the House of Representatives announced the creation of a bipartisan congressional caucus on burn pits, and a hearing on veterans' health issues is scheduled for June.

Congress has the power to direct the V.A. to presumptively grant disability benefits to veterans with lung disease if they were exposed to burn pits, but so far no member of Congress has proposed a bill to do so.

The Veterans of Foreign Wars is trying to change that. "For every generation's war, there is some toxic exposure," said Kenneth Wiseman, the V.F.W.'s associate legislative director. "In Vietnam it was Agent Orange. Then gulf war syndrome. Now burn pits." He said the V.F.W. is currently lobbying Congress to direct the V.A. to create a list of illnesses presumed to be caused by burn-pit exposure. The V.A. would grant disability benefits to any Iraq or Afghanistan veteran with a listed condition, so that "individuals don't have to assemble mountains of evidence one by one."

That is what Congress did for Vietnam veterans exposed to Agent Orange, but not until 1991 — 16 years after the Vietnam War ended, 22 years after a National Cancer Institute study demonstrated a link between Agent Orange and cancer in mice and 25 years after the scientist who helped invent the defoliant first sounded the alarm over its potential harmfulness to humans.

Arlington Cemetery, Nearly Full, May Become More Exclusive

BY DAVE PHILIPPS | MAY 28, 2018

To preserve space for future war heroes in the country's premier national cemetery, the Army is considering new rules that would turn away many currently eligible veterans.

ARLINGTON, VA. — The solemn ritual of a burial with military honors is repeated dozens of times a day, in foul weather or fair, at Arlington National Cemetery, honoring service members from privates to presidents. But in order to preserve the tradition of burial at the nation's foremost military cemetery for future generations, the Army, which runs Arlington, says that it may have to deny it to nearly all veterans who are living today.

At current burial rates, Arlington will be completely full in about 25 years. The Army, which manages the cemetery, wants to preserve space by tightening rules for who may be buried there.

Arlington is running out of room. Already the final resting place for more that 420,000 veterans and their relatives, the cemetery has been adding about 7,000 more each year. At that rate, even if the last rinds of open ground around its edges are put to use, the cemetery will be completely full in about 25 years.

"We're literally up against a wall," said Barbara Lewandrowski, a spokeswoman for the cemetery, as she stood in the soggy grass where marble markers march up to the stone wall separating the grounds from a six-lane highway. Even that wall has been put to use, stacked three high with niches for cremated remains.

The Army wants to keep Arlington going for at least another 150 years, but with no room to grow — the grounds are hemmed in by highways and development — the only way to do so is to significantly tighten the rules for who can be buried there. That has prompted a difficult debate over what Arlington means to the nation and how to balance egalitarian ideals against the site's physical limits.

The strictest proposal the Army is considering would allow burials only for service members killed in action or awarded the military's highest decoration for heroism, the Medal of Honor. Under those restrictions, Arlington would probably conduct fewer burials in a year than it does right now in a single week.

A policy like that would exclude thousands of currently eligible combat veterans and career officers who risked their lives in the service and who planned to be buried in Arlington among their fallen comrades.

"I don't know if it's fair to go back on a promise to an entire population of veterans," said John Towles, a legislative deputy director for Veterans of Foreign Wars who deployed to Iraq and Afghanistan. The group, with 1.7 million veterans, has adamantly opposed the new restrictions.

"Let Arlington fill up with people who have served their country," said Mr. Towles, who is eligible under current rules because he was wounded in battle. "We can create a new cemetery that, in time, will be just as special."

In Section 38, a tree has grown around a headstone for an infant who died in 1959.

Arlington is not the only place for military burials, of course. There are 135 national cemeteries maintained by the Department of Veterans Affairs across the country. But Arlington is by far the most prominent, and curtailing burial there would mean changing the site from an active cemetery into something closer to a museum.

The Army is conducting a survey of public opinion on the question through the summer, and expects to make formal recommendations in the fall.

"What does the nation want us to do?" Arlington's executive director, Karen Durham-Aguilera, said in an interview. "If the nation has the will to say we want to keep Arlington special and available, we have to make a change."

At current burial rates, Arlington will be completely full in about 25 years. The Army, which manages the cemetery, wants to preserve space by tightening rules for who may be buried there.

In a fitting turn of history, the cemetery now faced with a threat of overcrowding was created to address overcrowding. Early in the Civil War, the heavy death toll in battles near the capital soon filled Washington's existing cemeteries. Desperate for more burial space, the Quartermaster General of the Army, Montgomery C. Meigs, turned to a rolling green plantation just across the Potomac — the home of Gen. Robert E. Lee, whose decision to fight on the Confederate side marked him as a traitor in many Union eyes.

General Meigs's men began burying corpses beneath simple wood markers in the fields, and then, in a grim rebuke to the absent owner, lined the flower garden with the graves of Union officers and built a tomb near the door of the plantation house to hold the bones of 2,100 unknown dead.

At first, Arlington was anything but a coveted resting place. Most early burials were of ordinary soldiers whose families could not afford to have their remains shipped home. But as revered Union officers later chose to be buried in Arlington among the troops, the cemetery rose in prestige. The Tomb of the Unknowns was erected after World War I, and on nearly every Memorial Day since then, the sitting president has laid a wreath there.

Among the limestone rows are milestones of human progress: The first explorer to map the Grand Canyon, the first person killed in an airplane crash, the first astronauts to die trying to reach space. Some distinguished themselves on the battlefield, others in later life, including Albert Sabin, who served briefly as a wartime Army doctor and went on to develop a polio vaccine, and Oliver Wendell Holmes Jr., a wounded Civil War lieutenant of little distinction who later became a Supreme Court justice. Most would have been barred under restrictions now being contemplated by the Army.

The modern concept of Arlington — an egalitarian Elysian field where generals and G.I.'s of every creed and color are buried side by side — did not truly emerge until the cemetery was desegregated after World War II, according to Micki McElya, a history professor at the University of Connecticut who has written about the cemetery.

"Many look to the place as a self-evident case for national inclusion and belonging, as an expression of the many and diverse become one," Professor McElya said in an interview. That, she said, is the Arlington cited by Khizr Khan, the father of an Army captain killed in Iraq and buried at the cemetery, when he urged Donald J. Trump to visit.

"Look at the graves of brave patriots who died defending the United States of America," Mr. Khan said in his speech at the 2016 Democratic National Convention. "You will see all faiths, genders, and ethnicities."

Now, though, that all-inclusive idea is bumping up against the lack of space.

Arlington has tried to stretch what room it has. It ended the old practice of burying family members side by side, and now stacks them two or three deep in a single plot. In sections that hold only cremated remains, the rows are now spaced closer together. But planners say those measures can do only so much.

Under current rules, burial plots in Arlington are open to veterans who served long enough to retire from the military; to troops who were wounded in battle or received one of the three highest awards for valor; to prisoners of war; to troops who die while on active duty; and to a few civilians who serve in high-level government posts. Their spouses and dependents are also eligible.

The Army has laid out several proposals for changing those rules to keep Arlington open longer, but only the most restrictive options would make much difference — and those are the least popular among veterans.

"Everybody wants to see Arlington stay open," said Gerardo Avila, a wounded Iraq veteran who spoke to Congress on the issue on behalf of the American Legion. He said that while he would gladly give up his own spot to ensure a place for a future Medal of Honor recipient, the Legion, with 2.3 million members, does not share that view.

"You are voting your own rights away," he said. "I'm not sure our members are willing to do that."

Army surveys indicate that the public supports giving priority to troops killed in battle or awarded the Medal of Honor. But it is not hard to find graves in Arlington of arguably deserving men and women who did neither.

On a recent evening, Nadine McLachlan knelt before the grave of her husband, Col. Joseph McLachlan, to trim the grass with scissors before arranging a bright vase of lilies. Colonel McLachlan was a fighter pilot who strafed the beaches of Normandy on D-Day; a week after the invasion, he was shot down and, though wounded, made his way back through enemy lines to safety. He went on to fly more than 100 more missions, earning the Legion of Merit, the Distinguished Flying Cross and 17 Air Medals for acts of heroism in flight.

He survived the war and lived for six more decades, until 2005. So under the most restrictive proposals, he would not qualify for burial at Arlington.

"My Joe was a wonderful man — very courageous, very kind," Ms. McLachlan said. "I'm not sure that's fair, to cut out men like him. They were in the line of fire, even if they made it. Being buried here with his friends meant a lot to him. It really is a dilemma."

Glossary

&c. Alternative form of "etc;" short for "et cetera," which is Latin for "and so forth."

arsenal A collection of weapons and military equipment stored by the armed forces.

autonomous Something that functions separately or independently.

contingency A plan for an unseen event or circumstance.

cyber Having to do with the culture of computers, information technology and virtual reality.

deferment The postponement of a person's enlistment into the armed forces.

dependent A person who has to rely on another, especially a family member, for financial support.

deserter A person who leaves the armed forces without permission.

draft The act of being selected for the armed forces without the individual's consent.

enlistment The act of enrolling or being enrolled in the armed forces.

fleet A large group of ships controlled by the armed forces and acting together under the same command.

forensic Having to do with using scientific methods and techniques in an investigation.

inauguration The ceremony of formally admitting someone into an office or position.

induction The process of bringing someone into an organization or military service.

mission An important assignment or task carried out by a group of military personnel.

mobilize To assemble or prepare armed forces into readiness for active service or a mission.

politicize To make an action or event into something political.

recruitment The act of enlisting new people in the armed forces.

reserve Part of a military force held in readiness to continue an attack or defense made by the rest of the force.

task force An armed force organized to carry out a special mission or operation.

transgender Having to do with a person whose gender identity is inconsistent with the gender they were assigned at birth.

Media Literacy Terms

"Media literacy" refers to the ability to access, understand, critically assess and create media. The following terms are important components of media literacy, and they will help you critically engage with the articles in this title.

angle The aspect of a news story that a journalist focuses on and develops.

attribution The method by which a source is identified or by which facts and information are assigned to the person who provided them.

balance Principle of journalism that both perspectives of an argument should be presented in a fair way.

bias A disposition of prejudice in favor of a certain idea, person or perspective.

column A type of story that is a regular feature, often on a recurring topic, written by the same journalist, generally known as a columnist.

commentary A type of story that is an expression of opinion on recent events by a journalist generally known as a commentator.

credibility The quality of being trustworthy and believable, said of a journalistic source.

editorial Article of opinion or interpretation.

fake news A fictional or made-up story presented in the style of a legitimate news story, intended to deceive readers; also commonly used as an insult to criticize legitimate news because of its perspective or unfavorable coverage of a subject.

feature story Article designed to entertain as well as to inform.

human interest story Type of story that focuses on individuals and how events or issues affect their life, generally offering a sense of relatability to the reader.

impartiality Principle of journalism that a story should not reflect a journalist's bias and should contain balance.

interview story Type of story in which the facts are gathered primarily by interviewing another person or persons.

inverted pyramid Method of writing a story using facts in order of importance, beginning with a lead and then gradually adding paragraphs in order of relevance from most interesting to least interesting.

news story An article or style of expository writing that reports news, generally in a straightforward fashion and without editorial comment.

op-ed An opinion piece that reflects a prominent individual's opinion on a topic of interest.

paraphrase The summary of an individual's words, with attribution, rather than a direct quotation of their exact words.

quotation The use of an individual's exact words indicated by the use of quotation marks and proper attribution.

reliability The quality of being dependable and accurate, said of a journalistic source.

rhetorical device Technique in writing intending to persuade the reader or communicate a message from a certain perspective.

style A distinctive use of language in writing or speech; also a news or publishing organization's rules for consistent use of language with regards to spelling, punctuation, typography and capitalization, usually regimented by a house style guide.

tone A manner of expression in writing or speech.

Media Literacy Questions

1. In "The Dwindling of the Army and Its Causes" (on page 18), the author directly quotes Col. H. O. S. Heistand. What are the strengths of the use of a direct quote as opposed to a paraphrase? What are the weaknesses?

2. "Put War Service on Men of Class 1, Urges Crowder" (on page 25) features several charts. What do the charts add to the article?

3. What type of story is "Draft Board Drama" (on page 40)? Can you identify another article in this collection that is the same type of story?

4. Identify the various sources cited in the article "Pentagon Widens Rules to Prevent Racial Inequities" (on page 70). How does Dana Adams Schmidt attribute information to each of these sources in the article? How effective are Schmidt's attributions in helping the reader identify his sources?

5. "Seeking a Future in Military, Undeterred by Talk of War" (on page 80) is an example of an interview. What are the benefits of providing readers with direct quotes of an interviewed subject's speech? Is the subject of an interview always a reliable source?

6. Identify each of the sources in "Air Force Failed to Report Dozens of Service Members to Gun Database" (on page 104) as a primary source or a secondary source. Evaluate the reliability and credibility of each source. How does your evaluation of each source change your perspective on this article?

7. The article "The Warrior at the Mall" (on page 111) is an example of an op-ed. Identify how Phil Klay's attitude and tone help convey his opinion on the topic.

8. Compare the headlines of "Military Women, Too, Should Serve Unmolested" (on page 135) and "Reports of Sexual Assault in the Military Rise by 10 Percent, Pentagon Finds" (on page 140). Which is a more compelling headline, and why? How could the less compelling headline be changed to better draw the reader's interest?

9. Does "Pentagon Approves Gender-Reassignment Surgery for Service Member" (on page 162) use multiple sources? What are the strengths of using multiple sources in a journalistic piece? What are the weaknesses of relying heavily on only one source or a few sources?

10. Does Emily Cochrane demonstrate the journalistic principle of impartiality in her article "Forces Align Against a New Military Branch to 'Win Wars' in Space" (on page 171)? If so, how did she do so? If not, what could Cochrane have included to make her article more impartial?

11. What is the intention of the article "Suit Calls Navy Board Biased Against Veterans With PTSD" (on page 193)? How effectively does it achieve its intended purpose?

12. What type of story is "Veterans Go Back to Court Over Burn Pits. Do They Have a Chance?" (on page 198)? Can you identify another article in this collection that is the same type of story?

Citations

All citations in this list are formatted according to the
Modern Language Association's (MLA) style guide.

BOOK CITATION

THE NEW YORK TIMES EDITORIAL STAFF. *Military Service.* New York: New York
Times Educational Publishing, 2019.

ONLINE ARTICLE CITATIONS

BALDWIN, HANSON W. "The R.O.T.C. — II: Compulsory Aspect Cause of
Argument Within the Services and the Colleges." *The New York Times,*
23 Aug. 1960, https://timesmachine.nytimes.com/timesmachine/1960
/08/23/99791024.html.

BAUMGAERTNER, EMILY. "Morale, Allegiance and Drinking: How Military
Challenge Coins Evolved and Spread." *The New York Times,* 11 Apr. 2018,
https://www.nytimes.com/2018/04/11/us/politics/challenge-coins.html.

CARRNS, ANN. "Military Is Overhauling Its Retirement Systems." *The New
York Times,* 3 Nov. 2017, https://www.nytimes.com/2017/11/03/your-money
/military-pensions-thrift-savings-plan.html.

CHEN, DAVID W., AND SOMINI SENGUPTA. "Not Yet Citizens but Eager to Fight
for the U.S." *The New York Times,* 12 Oct. 2001, https://timesmachine
.nytimes.com/timesmachine/2001/10/26/865745.html.

COCHRANE, EMILY. "Forces Align Against a New Military Branch to 'Win Wars'
in Space." *The New York Times,* 26 July 2017, https://www.nytimes
.com/2017/07/26/us/politics/congress-budget-space-corps-pentagon
-opposition.html.

COOPER, HELENE. "Army, Struggling to Get Technology in Soldiers' Hands,
Tries the Unconventional." *The New York Times,* 18 Mar. 2018, https://www
.nytimes.com/2018/03/18/world/asia/us-army-futures-command
-technology.html.

COOPER, HELENE. "Critics See Echoes of 'Don't Ask, Don't Tell' in Military Transgender Ban." *The New York Times*, 28 Mar. 2018, https://www.nytimes.com/2018/03/28/us/politics/pentagon-transgender-ban-legal-challenges.html.

COOPER, HELENE. "Pentagon Approves Gender-Reassignment Surgery for Service Member." *The New York Times*, 14 Nov. 2017, https://www.nytimes.com/2017/11/14/us/politics/pentagon-transgender-surgery.html.

COOPER, HELENE. "Transgender People Will Be Allowed to Enlist in the Military as a Court Case Advances." *The New York Times*, 11 Dec. 2017, https://www.nytimes.com/2017/12/11/us/politics/transgender-military-pentagon.html.

CUTHBERT, ROB. "An Injustice in the Bergdahl Sentence." *The New York Times*, 3 Nov. 2017, https://www.nytimes.com/2017/11/03/opinion/bowe-bergdahl-sentence-benefits.html.

DAVIS, JULIE HIRSCHFELD, AND HELENE COOPER. "Trump Says Transgender People Will Not Be Allowed in the Military." *The New York Times*, 26 July 2017, https://www.nytimes.com/2017/07/26/us/politics/trump-transgender-military.html.

FAZIO, TERESA. "The Thickest Glass Ceiling in the Marine Corps Breaks." *The New York Times*, 25 Sept. 2017, https://www.nytimes.com/2017/09/25/opinion/marine-corps-women-.html.

FOUNTAIN, JOHN W. "Seeking a Future in Military, Undeterred by Talk of War." *The New York Times*, 22 Sept. 2001, https://timesmachine.nytimes.com/timesmachine/2001/09/22/303267.html.

GIBBONS-NEFF, THOMAS. "Reports of Sexual Assault in the Military Rise by 10 Percent, Pentagon Finds." *The New York Times*, 30 Apr. 2018, https://www.nytimes.com/2018/04/30/us/politics/sexual-assault-reports-military-increase.html.

GIBBONS-NEFF, THOMAS. "Training Quick and Staffing Unfinished, Army Units Brace for Surging Taliban." *The New York Times*, 26 Jan. 2018, https://www.nytimes.com/2018/01/26/world/asia/afghanistan-army-trainers.html.

GONZALEZ, DAVID. "Recruiters' New Obstacle: War Fear." *The New York Times*, 10 Dec 1990, https://timesmachine.nytimes.com/timesmachine/1990/12/10/589590.html.

HARP, SETH. "Veterans Go Back to Court Over Burn Pits. Do They Have a Chance?" *The New York Times*, 17 May 2018, https://www.nytimes.com/2018/05/17/magazine/burn-pits-veterans.html.

HEDGES, CHRIS. "In Dad's Footsteps, and Flight Suit." *The New York Times*, 19 Dec. 2002, https://timesmachine.nytimes.com/timesmachine/2002/12/19/460796.html.

IVES, MIKE. "A World War II Mystery Is Solved, and Emotions Flood In." *The New York Times*, 28 May 2018, https://www.nytimes.com/2018/05/28/world/asia/world-war-ii-bomber-mia-new-guinea.html.

JORDAN, MIRIAM. "Fast Track to Citizenship Is Cut Off for Some Military Recruits." *The New York Times*, 15 Sept. 2017, https://www.nytimes.com/2017/09/15/us/fast-track-to-citizenship-is-cut-off-for-some-military-recruits.html.

KLAY, PHIL. "The Warrior at the Mall." *The New York Times*, 14 Apr. 2018, https://www.nytimes.com/2018/04/14/opinion/sunday/the-warrior-at-the-mall.html.

MCNEIL, DONALD G., JR. "Should Women Be Sent Into Combat?" *The New York Times*, 21 July 1991, https://www.nytimes.com/1991/07/21/weekinreview/ideas-trends-should-women-be-sent-into-combat.html.

MILLER, JUDITH. "In Qatar, Forgotten U.S. Warriors Wait." *The New York Times*, 25 Dec. 1990, https://timesmachine.nytimes.com/timesmachine/1990/12/25/712290.html.

THE NEW YORK TIMES. "Army Will Try Out Would-Be Aviators." *The New York Times*, 13 Sept. 1930, https://timesmachine.nytimes.com/timesmachine/1930/09/14/102159749.html.

THE NEW YORK TIMES. "Dolling Up Our Army: Back to Blue and Gold Braid for Our Olive Drab Fighting Men — Perhaps." *The New York Times*, 13 May 1923, https://timesmachine.nytimes.com/timesmachine/1923/05/13/105862243.html.

THE NEW YORK TIMES. " 'Don't Ask, Don't Tell' Is Challenged in Suit." *The New York Times*, 8 Mar. 1994, https://www.nytimes.com/1994/03/08/us/don-t-ask-don-t-tell-is-challenged-in-suit.html.

THE NEW YORK TIMES. "Draft Board Drama." *The New York Times*, 18 May 1941, https://timesmachine.nytimes.com/timesmachine/1941/05/18/85494245.html.

THE NEW YORK TIMES. "The Dwindling of the Army and Its Causes." *The New York Times*, 22 Sept. 1907, https://timesmachine.nytimes.com/timesmachine/1907/09/22/104790306.html.

THE NEW YORK TIMES. "Gay Soldiers, Good Soldiers." *The New York Times*, 1 Sept. 1991, https://www.nytimes.com/1991/09/01/opinion/gay-soldiers-good-soldiers.html.

THE NEW YORK TIMES. "Put War Service on Men of Class 1, Urges Crowder." *The New York Times*, 3 Jan. 1918, https://timesmachine.nytimes.com /timesmachine/1918/01/04/102651818.html.

THE NEW YORK TIMES. "The United States Army: Report of Major General Scott." *The New York Times*, 22 Nov. 1852, https://timesmachine.nytimes .com/timesmachine/1852/12/15/87847445.html.

OPPEL, RICHARD A., JR. "Air Force Failed to Report Dozens of Service Members to Gun Database." *The New York Times*, 28 Nov. 2017, https://www .nytimes.com/2017/11/28/us/air-force-devin-kelley-gunman-texas.html.

PHILIPPS, DAVE. "Arlington Cemetery, Nearly Full, May Become More Exclusive." *The New York Times*, 28 May 2018, https://www.nytimes.com/2018 /05/28/us/arlington-cemetery-veterans.html.

PHILIPPS, DAVE. "For Transgender Service Members, a Mix of Sadness, Anger and Fear." *The New York Times*, 27 July 2017, https://www.nytimes.com /2017/07/26/us/for-transgender-service-members-a-mix-of-sadness-anger -and-fear.html.

PHILIPPS, DAVE. "Sergeant Sues Defense Dept. Over 'Outdated' H.I.V. Policies." *The New York Times*, 31 May 2018, https://www.nytimes.com/2018 /05/31/us/defense-department-sued-hiv-policy.html.

PHILIPPS, DAVE. "Suit Calls Navy Board Biased Against Veterans With PTSD." The New York Times, 2 Mar. 2018, https://www.nytimes.com/2018/03/02 /us/navy-ptsd-lawsuit.html.

ROSENBERG, MATTHEW, AND DAVE PHILIPPS. "All Combat Roles Now Open to Women, Defense Secretary Says." *The New York Times*, 3 Dec. 2015, https:// www.nytimes.com/2015/12/04/us/politics/combat-military -women-ash-carter.html.

RUTENBERG, AMY J. "How the Draft Reshaped America." *The New York Times*, 6 Oct. 2017, https://www.nytimes.com/2017/10/06/opinion/vietnam-draft .html.

SANGER, DAVID E. "Pentagon Puts Cyberwarriors on the Offensive, Increasing the Risk of Conflict." *The New York Times*, 17 June 2018, https://www .nytimes.com/2018/06/17/us/politics/cyber-command-trump.html.

SCHMIDT, DANA ADAMS. "Pentagon Widens Rules to Prevent Racial Inequities." *The New York Times*, 18 Dec. 1970, https://timesmachine.nytimes .com/timesmachine/1970/12/18/145971952.html.

SCHMITT, ERIC. "Navy Returns to Compasses and Pencils to Help Avoid Collisions at Sea." *The New York Times*, 27 Sept. 2017, https://www.nytimes

.com/2017/09/27/us/politics/navy-orders-safety-operational-standards
.html.

SHPIGEL, BEN. "Buoyed by Financial Support, Military Veterans Are a Growing Part of the Paralympics." *The New York Times*, 18 Mar. 2018, https://
www.nytimes.com/2018/03/18/sports/paralympics-military-veterans.html.

TACKETT, MICHAEL. "From Annapolis to Congress? These Three Women Know
Tough Missions." *The New York Times*, 29 Jan. 2018, https://www.nytimes
.com/2018/01/29/us/politics/women-annapolis-democrats-congress-trump
.html.

TRUSSELL, C. P. "Army, Navy to Back Work-or-Fight Law for All Men 18 to 45."
The New York Times, 8 Jan. 1945, https://timesmachine.nytimes.com
/timesmachine/1945/01/09/88177032.html.

UFFORD, MATT. "15 Years Ago, I Helped Start a War That Hasn't Ended."
The New York Times, 20 Mar. 2018, https://www.nytimes.com/2018/03/20
/magazine/iraq-war-invasion-15-years.html.

VENKATESAN, SUPRIYA. "Military Women, Too, Should Serve Unmolested."
The New York Times, 18 Oct. 2017, https://www.nytimes.com/2017/10/18
/opinion/military-women-molested.html.

Index

This book is current up until the time of printing. For the most up-to-date reporting, visit www.nytimes.com.